I0427113

TANDOORI TEXAN TALES

By

Raj Doré

© 2003 by Raj Doré. All rights reserved.

No part of this book may be reproduced, stored in a retrieval system, or transmitted by any means, electronic, mechanical, photocopying, recording, or otherwise, without written permission from the author.

ISBN: 1-4107-6999-2 (e-book)
ISBN: 1-4107-6998-4 (Paperback)

Library of Congress Control Number: 2003094864

This book is printed on acid free paper.

Printed in the United States of America
Bloomington, IN

1stBooks - rev. 10/24/03

CONTENTS

THE CELEBRITY

CHAPTER 1

It all started with American Airlines Flight 523 at the Dallas/Fort Worth International Airport. Seema, my wife dropped me off at the Terminal A by the curbside at 3:30PM on that Sunday afternoon, and drove off before it was going to be Munni's feed time.

I was on my weekly jaunt to Raleigh, North Carolina. I had one leg here and one leg there. I was working on a project to provide Software Consultancy to Carolina Power & Utility Company, while my home was still in Dallas.

I was called a Contract Consultant. Large corporations would often hire people like me to help them out with sudden surge of work. While they needed extra hands to get over such humps, they loathed hiring permanent employees.

Permanent employees would need extra cost to part with, when it was time to bid them good bye. Stockholders would also be quite pleased that the total payroll was kept low. This was of course a fallacy. The cost came back to them by way of revolving door when the same personnel were called in as hourly contractors, like me. For me working as an independent contractor brought a higher income while I took the risk of not finding work between two contracts.

I had to rent an apartment in Raleigh for the duration of this 6-month project that had now extended to over a year. I would fly home every Friday night and get back to the Project, on Sunday night. On some weekends Seema and Munni would fly down to Raleigh as well. They could not do that all the time due to Seema's job in Dallas or her sheer unwillingness.

The skycap politely informed me that curbside check-in for baggage was put on hold that evening due to a security alert. 'Security Alert', oh my God how many times have I had to put up with that phrase. Would life ever get back to its normalcy of 2 years ago? Those Al-Qaida guys had surely got the whole country topsy-turvy.

As I kept mumbling to myself, I swished my Visa into the Cart-smart and pulled out a handcart. I loaded my luggage on to it and slowly started pushing it toward the escalator. As usual there was a long line of frustrated passengers trying to get through the Security Check. After standing in the rear for a few minutes I felt even more exasperated at the slowness of the movement in front of me. Only way I found some solace was by looking over my shoulders and

4

seeing how long the line had grown behind me. Life itself is like that, is it not? If only you look at people more unfortunate than you are, you feel yourself not so unlucky after all.

The whole process did finally come grindingly to an end. After checking the stuff in and going through the turnstiles, I found that I still had a good 45 minutes for the Flight.

I was glad I had the membership to the American Airlines' Admirals Club. This is a small little niche where you can rise above the dust and din of travelling crowds. You realize its importance if you are constantly living out of your suitcase and running along miles and miles of airport conveyor belts, for making a living. For a mere $350 per year you can buy an entry to this home between your homes.

There are always those charming hostesses with smiling faces that politely first ask you to show your membership card. Having established your identity, they take you into their wings. There are spacious areas for relaxing, reading, watching TV or just do nothing. If you are a business traveler like me, you can even hook up your laptop and catch up with your reports due next morning. There are soft lights, music and a bar for someone needing uplifting of spirits, literally.

At about 5 minutes before the Boarding time, I gathered my hand baggage and got through the gangway into the waiting aircraft. There was again a long line of people on the aisle trying to shove their hand luggage on to the bin overhead and squeezing their way into the appropriate seats. Then there were those moms trying to manage a few unruly brats in one hand and some baggage on the other.

My seat, as I had requested while making the booking, was fortunately on the aisle side of one of the front rows. I settled down quickly and strapped myself.

Once the Flight Crew cleared the aisles after serving what passes off as evening snacks, I felt like stretching myself a little. Since the toilets on the rear were too far, I thought I would use the ones in the front. I passed through the First Class cabin. After refreshing myself, I languidly started walking back. Then what transpired changed rest of my life.

The First Class was very sparsely occupied, just two or three people in all those 20 odd seats. I spotted one face that struck my solar plexus like a ton of bricks. She was wearing *Salvar-kameez* and had covered a good portion of her head with the *Dupatta*. She pretended to be engrossed in a book, quite oblivious of the surroundings. The setting sun shone through the window on her side. She was wearing very large sunglasses that covered almost one-third of her face. Very obviously, she valued her privacy very dearly and did not want to be recognized. Even then, it struck me that she seemed very familiar, as if I might have met her some where, some time. But I just could not place a label on that face. I kept walking and came back to my seat.

The sun had set after a while. The lights had been dimmed. Only some soft lights at the aisle were kept on. Some passengers had turned on their reading lights. I stood up and walked toward the First Class cabin once again, wanting to take another look at this mysterious passenger. The reading light illuminated her face partially; it was still buried in the book. Only then slowly, it all came back to me.

She was Archana Roy. Yes, oh my God! It was indeed she. I had watched her on the movie screen so many times.

My first reaction was to want to walk up to her and ask if it was really she. If I had still been in my college days, I might have done it. I have done it with several celebrities while in the University. If nothing else, at least ask for an autograph and show proudly to my friends. My collection of autographs included stars from several walks of life, Cricketers, Statesmen, visiting celebrity Speakers at the College functions and yes, Movie Stars.

But now things were so different, after having entered real workaday world. It seemed so silly for somebody to do that at my station in life. You are less inclined to take the risk of your pride being hurt. Besides, it was so obvious to me that she was quite insistent on not being recognized. I gave up that whole idea.

I continued cranking on my laptop keyboard. This report was due at 10:00AM next morning. If I were not ready with it for the presentation at the Staff Meeting, Don Welsner, the Project Manager would chew me alive. Release of funds for the whole Project depended upon our convincing the Departmental Heads of our capabilities at meeting the goals. Getting involved in hobnobbing with movie stars wanting to remain anonymous was way down on my list of priorities.

Usually I schedule these periodic trips home at least a month ahead of time. But my trip previous week had to be rescheduled for this week, at the last minute. Don had insisted that I stay back and get the Payroll System's conversion fully tested before I left. It had been impossible for me to get a direct flight from Dallas to Raleigh. The best I could do was this flight, hopping via Little Rock, Arkansas and Atlanta, Georgia.

The Little Rock Airport is a relatively small wayside airport with much fewer facilities. The stopover was for some 45 minutes. Some of us got down to walk around in the airport. I gathered my briefcase, shoulder bag and the laptop. Then came out of the plane slowly walking down the gangway.

As I was browsing at the gift shop, I looked through the corner of my eyes. She had also got down and was browsing at another corner of the shop. The lounge was inside the Secure Area and I wanted to remain within that. I did not find anything interesting at the shop. I settled down at a lounge chair and resumed working on the report.

However I saw that she had wandered out of the secure area, possibly to look around other shops outside.

Some ten minutes before boarding time, I once again put all of my stuff together to get back into the flight. As I passed along the boarding gate, I heard some altercation near the Security Check area. Curious as to what could it be, I looked around to find that the Security Guard was having some heated arguments with her. There was obviously some problem as she was trying to get back through the Security Check.

I might have kept walking, minding my own business. As luck would have it, I came toward the scene of disturbance and volunteered to intervene. The Security people were keen that she be strip searched and thoroughly examined as they considered her a security risk. She on the other hand was quite insistent that she should not be put to any such humiliation.

As it happens in most such instances, there was also probably plenty of communication gaps. She conversing in her convent educated British accent and they trying to convey their thoughts in heavy Southern flair. As there were plenty of people waiting behind her to get in, the scene of altercation was moved into another location while the rest of the passengers were allowed to keep moving.

The other location happened to be the office of Sergeant Steve McKlusky, as it was announced on the brass plate outside its door. There was a glass panel that secluded the office from rest of the lounge, making it possible for outsiders to see but not hear, what was going on within. Sergeant McKlusky was the Chief Security Officer of the Airport. He was not in the chamber at that time. There were Officers Pete Williams and Maria Hernandez. The former was an African American while the latter, a Hispanic young lady. They were trying to interrogate her in all possible ways and she was being defiant.

I knocked on the door, slowly opened it and literally stuck my neck into that confrontation. I smiled and looked at Officer Williams and said "Officer, there seems to be some problem here. Could you use some help?" He readily smiled back and said, "Thanks very much for asking Sir. Yes, we sure can use some help. Please step in."

They explained to me that they were under a very high alert of Security threat that day and were totally unwilling to take any chances whatsoever. I wondered if they focussed their suspicion on her due to her attire and looks. But decided not to exacerbate the situation by kicking in more controversy.

I spoke out, "Officers, I quite realize you are doing your duty and doing it very well. As a matter of fact, we as passengers feel so much more confident of travelling because of good Officers like you. She already went through one Security Check while boarding at Dallas, is it not? Please let me tell you further that, I am Dr. Rohit Sharma holding a Ph.D., in Computer Engineering from the Cockerell-Hill University of Dallas, Texas. I am a U.S. Citizen currently flying to Raleigh North Carolina on an assignment to provide software design to the Carolina Power & Light on their Nuclear Security System. Please allow me assure you that this young lady is no potential or real Terrorist. You could safely let her go."

Officer Maria Hernandez spoke first. "Thank you Sir. However, you have not established what is her relationship with you and how could you be so sure of her".

"Could both of you please step into the ante-room with me? I would like to show you something in private. Please close the door behind you", I replied.

I opened my briefcase and pulled out the latest edition of "News India Times", a sister publication of "The Times of India", coming out of New York City. I flipped to the 9th page. On the one side it had a large picture of Archana Roy being crowned Miss Universe from a couple of years ago. On the another side there was her picture receiving the Urvashi (The Most Outstanding Actress of the Year) Award from the President of India. There was a write up on her as well.

I showed it to them and told them, "You guys are making a big mistake. I strongly suggest you drop the whole case and quietly back off. Otherwise there is going to be plenty of ugly publicity for everybody, especially you. If you wish, you may call Sergeant McKlusky at home and ask. If it would help, I am willing to call Senator Jesse Helms of North Carolina and let his staff talk to you. I doubt whether that is the route you all wish to take."

There was a stunned silence for a couple of minutes. I closed the briefcase and walked out of the room, back into the lounge. I saw her coming out of the room as well.

American Airlines Flight 523 had taken off in the meantime without us. There was another flight via Minneapolis reaching Raleigh at 2AM. Even that was full and I was going to be 15th on the waiting list, not a good chance, by any means.

My first concern was my 10 O'clock meeting next morning 900 miles away. If I did not show up with that report, Don Wilsner would cut me into pieces and eat raw with his salad for lunch. I called him from the nearest telephone kiosk. Thank God, I was able to get through.

His little daughter picked up the phone and told me that her dad was watching his Alma Mater, UNC playing Nebraska in the Final Six of NCAA Basketball. I asked her how was UNC faring so far. Not too good, she said. That means Don was going to be in a sullen mood. When he finally came on the line, I asked him if anyway the meeting could be postponed by 24 hours. After some grumbling and groaning, he said he would check with his boss and call me back. In another half an hour my cell phone rang. Yes that was going to be okay.

CHAPTER 2

I did not want to take any more chances with flights. Only way I could be sure of reaching, even 24 hours later was to rent a car and drive all the way. I was at the Avis counter waiting anxiously for them to check out availability of some decent Wheels.

I saw her walking toward me. She smiled. Extending her hand, she said, "Thank you so very much. You saved me from a very ugly embarrassment". I asked her not to mention it at all. Then I asked her, what her further plans were? Whither was she heading next?

She was stuck from reaching her destination as well. What was worse, she did not have even the wherewithal that I had grabbed out of the deserting aircraft. As it turned out, her wallet with money and credit cards were all left on board the flight that was 35,000 feet above mother Earth. All she had got down with, was her handbag with her passport, travel papers and some small money stuck in one of its pockets.

I wanted to help and asked further. Did she know anybody here or elsewhere that she could call? Would she wish to use my calling card?

As it turned out, she had an aunt in New Jersey. When she called them, they had gone for the weekend and had not returned yet. She left a message on their answering machine. She had nowhere else to go as she loathed asking anybody else especially the business contacts. I told her of my plans and offered her a ride, if she wished to hitch hike with me. She seemed to have little better alternative.

After checking my Driver License and Credit Card, Avis made me sign the rental papers. What we got was a green Toyota Camry, 4-door sedan. I threw my few belongings in the back seat. I strapped myself in the driver seat and opened the door on the other side for her to get in. By about 7:30PM Central Time, we were on our way. I tried keeping cool with my companion and concentrated on driving.

She broke the ice and came clean. She said, "I know very well that you know who I am. But there is very little I know about you, excepting what you told those Security Cops. Why not we stop pretending and become friends?"

I told her, "Yes I do know who you are. As a matter of fact, you may even count me amongst your countless fans. But you see I am a regular middle class Professional. My Universe and yours can hardly ever intersect. The last thing I want is a celebrity movie star turning my simple life topsy-turvy. Let us just downgrade our relationship from friendship to acquaintance. Once we reach Raleigh, I will see to it that you can get to wherever you wish to go safely. If you wish you might repay me whenever you can. That is all there is to it, between you and me. Our paths will never cross again, I am quite sure."

"Never say never. Besides, please don't be too harsh on yourself or me. Just hang loose and treat me like any other girl next door. As for repaying, I may never be able to repay for what you did for me today", she said.

"Okay let us compromise. We will not put a label on our relationship. Let us be whatever comes naturally to us. As for repayment, I will take a rain check".

We passed a huge billboard inviting us to Hope, Arkansas, the birthplace of Ex-President Bill Clinton just 5 miles away. But we were hardly in the mood to go gallivanting on sightseeing missions and collecting souvenirs. We had a very long drive ahead of us.

I was on U.S. Highway 40 speeding toward the Northeast at a good 70-mph. On an average I can clock about a mile a minute. I break after every one hour for a little stretching and freshening up at Little Boys' Room. I am never comfortable driving all through the night. So I stop overnight to get a comfortable night's sleep. Next morning, I always fill the gas tank of my car and myself with a hearty breakfast, before heading further. Who knows when is the next place where we would get either?

As you cross the bridge over the Mississippi River, on US-40, you not only cross state-boundaries from Arkansas into Tennessee, but also go right into the city of Memphis. You can also see the difference in the standards of maintaining highways between the two states.

Memphis would be the last major city for quite some distance of our journey. Since neither my companion nor me had much by way of personal belongings, I thought it would make sense to halt at a Department Store before they close for the day and buy ourselves some articles of clothing, toiletries and other bare necessities.

As we were driving out of Memphis, it had become quite dark. She just tilted her seat backwards and closed her eyes. There were just those green lights of various dials on the dashboard. There was not much traffic on the highway. Just an 18-wheeler every once in a while that I had to overtake. To break the eerie silence, I turned on the radio. I caught a station of University of Memphis, playing some great jazz.

Suddenly the music stopped and a voice announced late breaking news. "This is AP Network News. American Airlines Flight 523 bound from Dallas/Fort Worth to Raleigh, North Carolina has lost contact with the control tower, after taking off from Little Rock, Arkansas. We are still monitoring the news and will keep you updated." We were startled at first. But denial took over our attitude. We told ourselves, everything must be alright. It must be one of those incidents that end up being a 'technical' problem with radar or communication. As we were driving away from Memphis, there was no good station that we could catch, to get updated on that disturbing news.

This route is very familiar to me. I have plied on it several times in the past year. There is this little town 300 miles from Little Rock, at the outskirts of Nashville, where there is a ranch of Country Singer Loretta Lynn, of "Coal Miner's Daughter" fame. They hold Country & Western music concerts there, every so often. It has a quaint little restaurant. The waitresses with sizable bosoms, wearing dark flowered frocks, with embroidered aprons, attend to you with gleeful smiles. The tablecloths in red and white checks are nicely starched. There are little baskets of fresh baked buns wrapped in spotlessly white napkins. You can get a hearty dinner buffet of fried-chicken, roast beef, gravy, mashed potato, beans and what have you, for $10.99. After the dinner you may browse in the gift shop looking at Loretta Lynn's artifacts whether or not you buy any souvenirs.

There is a cluster of 2 or 3 motels at reasonable prices, around this ranch. There is one owned by Gujrati émigrés from East Africa. This time again I was going to halt overnight in this little town like in previous instances. I find these little towns in the interior of the country extremely fascinating. That is where you get the flavor of real America from the sons and daughters of the soil, not at Hiltons and Sheratons of large Megalopolis.

By the time we pulled into the motel after our dinner, it was close to 10:30 at night. I let her stay in the car while I went to register, lest she be recognized. It was the same old Mrs. Suman Patel who greeted me with 'Aujo, kemcho', routine. We got two adjacent rooms inter-connected by a door.

As I was taking off my heavy shoes, I clicked on the remote to turn on the TV. It was by now all over the place. American Airlines Flight 523 had gone up in flames, an apparent act of hijacking and terrorism.

I heard a gentle knock on the intermediate door. She had seen the news on her TV as well. She was flushed pink and visibly shaken. She was in tears. She pleaded if she could come in, as she was scared and shocked beyond belief. I let her come in. We were both still in the same clothes we had been in all day.

We sat on the bed resting our backs on the pillow and headboard. We were watching the breaking news, clasping our hands with horror in our eyes. I could feel that she wanted to clasp me and hold me close. But I was just too confused and emotionally broken myself to make any kind of physical response to her overtures.

I somberly told her, "You have already repaid me more than what you ever owed me".

If ever there was a hairbreadth escape of my life, this was it. Instead of minding my own business and boarding that flight, I had decided to intervene in her imbroglio. That just saved my life.

It was getting close to midnight. I broke the silence and told her that we should now retire for the night and try to get some sleep. I slowly released my hand from her clasp. We had a long day ahead. It was imperative that we be on the highway by 7:00 AM, duly breakfasted and with a full tank of gas. Coffee & doughnuts would be served free, at the motel lobby starting 6:00 am.

She asked if she could leave the intermediate door open. I readily agreed. As she went into her room she turned and told me over her shoulder to give her a wake up call at 5:30, if she was not already awake.

I picked up the phone and called home. At home before going to bed, we normally turn off the telephone ring and let all the calls go to the answering machine. I was sure Seema would have done the same now. Before she got the morning news, I wanted her to know that I was not on the plane that blew up. I left the message. Then went into my bathroom to wash up and change. I came back, slipped into my sheets and turned off the bedside light.

I could see that her bathroom door was also half-ajar. I could see her full image reflected on the large mirror at the sink. She was probably unaware of that or she might have purposely wanted it that way.

She took her *Dupatta* and hung it on the peg at the opposite wall. Then she slowly removed the hooks on the back of her

Kameez one by one and slowly slid it over her head. Turned around and hung that also on the peg. She was wearing a flesh colored lacy bra. It covered her breasts only partially at the bottom with the two cups connected by a strip of lace. The upper fringe of the cups grazed through her chocolate brown nipples, showing a deep cleavage. She put her two hands behind her back and unhooked the bra. The straps came sliding over her shoulders and hands all the way out. Her two beautiful breasts wriggled out of the cups completely. They still had slight wrinkles from being harnessed, and the nipples were mildly upright. She then unfastened her Salwar and pulled it down her ankles. She had slender flat abdomen with cute little navel. Below that she was wearing a thin gauzy panty barely covering a well-manicured tuft of hair between the thighs. She had well-rounded hips. The cheeks were almost totally exposed as the seat of the panty had slid down into the valley in between. Her ivory complexion and smooth skin made her look like Neptune under moonlight.

She pulled out a brush from her handbag, stroked her dark brown hair a few times. She took out an elastic band and bound her hair into a ponytail. Then she splashed her face with cold running water. Rubbed some soap all over to remove the makeup. She rinsed her face finally and covered it with fresh laundered hand towel from the rack. Her clean spotless natural skin without any makeup shone looking even prettier.

Then she pulled out a brown paper package from the handbag and removed a T-shirt. She pulled it over her head and let it fall all the way down to her ankles. It was a top-to-

toe large T-shirt with "Welcome to Arkansas" written on the back with a picture of a sunrise behind Ozark Mountains in the front. Obviously this was the piece of article that had started the whole rigmarole that evening. Or should I say it was the cause of our survival today. I heard her switch off the light and get into her bed.

Oh Man! What a day! The day started off like any other day. By the end of it, I had not only survived death but also got to share very intimate moments with one of the most beautiful women in the world. The day was one of extremes in emotion. It had its Nadir and Zenith, so to say. Never a dull moment, for sure. I tried very hard to catch some sleep.

We started off as planned. By 7:00 AM I was speeding away on US-40 toward North Carolina. It was a cool morning and the sun felt quite nice. We opened the hood on top and let fresh morning air blow over our faces and hair. She took out her large sunglasses and covered her beautiful blue eyes. I also had mine on. It was a good 600 more miles to my apartment in Raleigh. I wanted to reach there before sunset.

We had crossed into the Eastern Time zone. While being between any two towns, one can hardly catch any radio station with good enough reception, FM or AM. That is why I carry some cassettes along, when on a long journey. But this time it was different. This was no trip that was forecast. I got tired of flipping from one bad station to another. I finally turned the radio off. There were some minutes of no sounds, only reverie.

She broke the silence and said, "I heard you call your home and leave a message. Is Seema your wife?"

I said, "Yes".

"Any children?" she asked.

"One 2-year old Munni. Aparna for real name", I said. And then blurted out, "She is the one that is still holding us together. For how long more, I wouldn't know".

"Where are you from in India?" she continued after remaining silent for a few moments.

Obviously she did not want to appear like she was prying into my rocky matrimony. Instead of going down that alley of conversation, she had changed the direction quite adroitly. I liked that.

CHAPTER 3

Our family had been living in Jabalpur for generations. We had our family farm there. My dad had gone to St. Stephens College in Delhi and graduated with a Master's degree in Economics. He had plans of going to London School of Economics further. Instead, with some helping hand from my grandfather, who was in the ICS, he got into a Dutch multi-national Oil corporation as a Management Trainee. After being with them for nearly 30 years, he retired as a Director, with the usual gold watch to commemorate it. He was still on their Board when he passed away 4 years ago.

Since my dad's was a transferable job including overseas assignments, my parents decided to put me into Doon School when I was 8. I used to spend my holidays with them or my grandparents or both, whichever was easier at that time. After passing my High School, I also attended St. Stephens College in Delhi, following my dad's and big brother's footsteps. But I graduated with a degree in Physics, Mathematics and Chemistry. Then I got a degree in Electrical Engineering from Roorki Engineering College.

My only sibling, an older brother Mukesh, graduated from St. Stephens with a Master's in History. Then he followed my grandfather's footsteps and got into the IAS, when that still had a lot of glitter and charm. He was always the more traditional, steady and responsible of us two. His was a well-charted textbook style path of life. He also got married to a very charming girl Nirmala with traditional family values. It was a marriage arranged by the families. They have a son Nirmal and a daughter Sunanda, still in schools.
He spent a couple of years in Geneva, Switzerland on a short stint with the United Nations before being posted as a Secretary to one of the major ministries at the Central Government.

After the passing away of dad, my mom was staying with them in Delhi. Despite all her foreign travels, she never liked living in the U.S., with us. She had come here a few times on short visits, but found the life here suffocating. Then there was all that humiliation one had to go through with the U.S. Consulate in obtaining the Visa. I tried visiting her at least once in a couple of years.

While still awaiting my results of the final exam at Roorki, I had started applying for post-graduate studies in the U.S., like most of my friends and colleagues. That took some time to fructify.

On graduating from the Engineering College, I did get picked up by a British company for a job in Calcutta. Even as my papers for going to the U.S. were being processed, I had already started seeing cracks in my career with this company. One day I had serious disagreement with my Manager who complained about me to the Director. I was called into his chamber and asked to tender official apology. On my refusal to do so, I was promptly given notice of dismissal. I walked out of that place with my chin high up. I was full of youthful pride and idealism.

Life at CHU, as Cockerell-Hill University in Dallas, Texas is called, started quite well. My dad had provided me with enough wherewithal to carry on the first Semester. Later I managed to get a teaching assistantship. There was also subsidized student housing on the campus. I shared a two bedroom apartment with Srinivas, a Chemistry Major. Altogether I just scraped by with some money left for fun as well.

'Fun' for most part meant some of us Indian boys getting together in the apartment of one of us, watching Indian movies on the video and drown plenty of beer. We would also share in preparing the food. Either we would bring something or pitch in preparing a curry or *sambaar*.

There were also TVs and VCRs individually with each of us. If you had those and could rent X-rated videos you must belong to the better off elite. If not, you had to make do with 'Penthouse' and 'Playboy', which gave more excitement than a new arrival from India could easily handle. That was as far as love life went for most guys.

The campus was quite segregated and stratified, in terms of color, ethnicity and cultural background, even though it was not 'Politically Correct' to officially acknowledge that. There was of course the stratification of Faculty and different layers of academic standings.

At the top echelon belonged boys and girls of Texan Oil Barons who drove about in Mercedes Benz and BMWs. They were there to show some degree of literacy before taking over their dad's business and riches. They partied and frolicked amongst themselves. The Texan girls are some of the most gorgeous looking in the world. That made it even more frustrating for the outsiders with whom they would mix as much as oil with water.

Then there were puddles of people from different backgrounds like Red China, Korea and the Middle-east, that would mingle amongst themselves. They also came from different economic strata from their own countries.

Kareem Al-Saeed was the son of a Kuwaiti Sheikh. He got an allowance of $40,000.00 per year from his dad. He lived in a well-furnished apartment and sported very expensive clothes and haircut. It was a common tale that he would bring home girls and have romantic evenings. He loved sipping some nice brew in front of his fireplace with soft music playing in the background. Even in the middle of Texas summer when the mercury would be hovering at 100+, he would turn on the fireplace with air-conditioning turned to full blast. But even with this kind of money Kareem could hardly make any headway with the local girls. Texan Oil would not mix with Kuwaiti Oil either. It took more than that. As a result he had to drive out in his convertible to Harry Hines Boulevard at dusk and look alongside the curb for a good hourly bargain.

On the other end of the scale was Cai from Red China who was the Teaching Assistant for Dr. Hegde of Chemistry Department. Cai had to maintain an "A" average to stay on the Financial Aid. Dr. Hegde originally from Mangalore, South Kanara in India, was a tenured professor. That meant in the name of 'Academic Freedom', he could not be shaken from his position of power by anything less than a Congressional Impeachment. He had made it through to this position with a lot of hardship. And now it was his turn. It was a common knowledge that he made Cai wash dishes, do grocery and laundry for his wife, as a part of academic exercises. Cai was a person of very modest means but with a very good-looking wife. She was known to do sewing and stitching for other students to make some extra buck. You could also make her go some 'extra length' for a few extra bucks, if you wanted.

Then there was this Dr. Margaret Stich, Professor of the Computer Science Department. She might have as well called herself Margaret Thatcher. Just like Dr. Hegde, she had a lot of pent up anger with this World. She had made it through this far in a Man's World suffering plenty of humiliation and injustice. She was willing to take on any male thing that moves with cudgels soaked in blood. If you were a male and one of her wards, you had to take a number and stand outside her door. Whenever she opened the door and let you in, you had to prove yourself innocent before she finished chewing that bit of apple she had just bitten. Or else, the next bite would be of your scalp. It was told, for a hobby and recreation, over the weekends she fixes an M1-tank parked in her backyard. She wanted to prove to all those Male Chauvinist Pigs at Pentagon that she could do a better job of fighting the Soviets than 5-star Generals. Soviet Union dissolved itself on hearing this.

There were the Fraternities and Sororities, into which the non-American, especially Indian students rarely participated because they firmly held that this kind of Western social life was immoral. They were here just to study and keep their cultural torch aloft all the time.

Amongst the South-Asian students, including India, Pakistan, Bangladesh & Sri Lanka, the gender ratio was something like 2 girls to 100 boys. Statistically there was a good probability that 1.95 of the 2 girls were already married. The remaining 0.05 would be the typical Gujju Behnji type. Of course these two categories are not mutually exclusive, plenty of them belonged to both.

Even amongst the boys, there were different types. Plenty came from little towns like Kumbakonam, who would do their 'Sandhyavandanam' and proudly go about with a spot of Vibhuti on their forehead. For them date was some dry fruit you could eat with a glass of milk. There were just a few guys that had experienced some kind of dame chasing and socializing in Bombay or Delhi.

Indians definitely had an edge over students from some other countries like China, Japan, Korea and even South America, due to their familiarity with the English language.

It was quite heart rending how those other boys and girls had to work 10 times harder to keep their grades and stay on the course.

It was common knowledge that Gigi was not one of those typical Texas girls. She was from Florida and would condescend talking to specimens of other ilk. She was in our Project Team. I took some courage and made the first move of asking her telephone number. I was just testing the waters if there was any long-term prospects for a social life. I was able to make it through the first hurdle. But invariably any time I called her either the line was busy or the call went through to an answering machine. Next time I met her, what the heck, I jumped right ahead and asked her out, using the first trick on the book.

"Have you ever tasted Indian cuisine? I know this fine Indian Restaurant. I wonder if you would want to discuss this assignment there this Saturday evening. It's due Monday, you know?"

Plomp came the response, "I would really love to do that, Roe-hitt. But this Saturday I am going out with my boyfriend Leff". A couple of nights later I was working late at the Computer Lab and there she was smooching some guy, definitely not Leff.

They all had this trump card up their sleeves. If they did not like the looks of you, they would pull this 'boyfriend' routine and say 'we can always be good friends'. In other words, 'Keep those candies and flowers coming. But I am not going to bed with you in this lifetime. I am waiting for Robert Redford in a red sports car'.

On that Holiday Season, Srinivas and I decided to call another girl Melissa who seemed to be quite nice and friendly. We planned a cozy evening at our place. We were going to cook some nice Indian meal. Have some drinks and music etc. Who knows who would be found wearing the Pajama Top next morning?

Since we were two of us, we told Melissa to come with a friend. Much to our excitement, she readily agreed. When that grand evening finally came, at the appointed time there was the doorbell. When I opened the door, there she was, Melissa giving a great smile with another guy.

They drank our expensive bottle of Chardonnay, ate our food, spilled curry on the carpet, filled the ashtray to overflowing and went away at 9:30PM to another discotheque by themselves leaving us behind. Our apartment looked like a war zone. We two had to clean up all day next day.

There were also some of those girls who had a well-determined menu card. You could buy yourself a kiss for a normal homework assignment. For serious help with Projects you could negotiate some heavy petting. For anything more than that, you had to do something really important like getting a Hot Ticket for a Bon Jovi concert.

Keeping a 'B' average in 2 semesters was compulsory. Otherwise you would be given the boot. The faculty was quite aware of how grades could be bought and sold amongst boys and girls. They would devise different means to put a check. There would be 'Surprise Quiz', 'Open Book' and 'Closed Book' exams and Projects. Students would always try to beat the system one way or another. After all Faculties consist of humans as well. It is these same students who later become Faculty. Don't they?

All in all the system here was better than what I was used to in India. There we used to kill ourselves in the last few months before the Final Exams. Two or four years' worth of work was being tested in a matter of 3 hours. Which was a very unfair way to judge, prize or penalize plenty of hard work. It was more a test of memorizing capabilities than knowledge. That way many a good life has been ruined or undeserving rewarded.

I finished my Master's in Computer Engineering in less than 2 years of arriving here. We had our Commencement Ceremony with throwing of hoods up in the air and all the jubilation. It was a sweet and sour moment. There was a sense of accomplishment and concern.

Soon after that, Reality started seeping. My student visa was going to expire in about 6 months. I still did not have a job. The job market for my skills was quite bad. Market was flushed with people like me. There was that periodic downturn in the Economy. Even corporations like IBM were laying off personnel and announcing hiring freeze. When a giant like IBM cuts back, it has a ripple effect all over the job market.

There were people with the much-prized Green Card or U.S. Citizenship staying home expecting the phone to ring. What chance did I have, with just a Student Visa? Quite religiously, I was mailing my resume to at least half a dozen destinations every day. Majority of them did not bother even to respond. Some would send a curt and crisp letter very neatly printed saying that my resume would be kept in their data-base for another 6 months, should any suitable opening arise.

That summer morning I walked up to Mrs. Barbara Allyson. She was the secretary of our Dean and Chairman of Computer Engineering Department, Dr. David Kennington.

I was wearing a red and blue T-shirt with CHU's mascot donkey on the back and a large embroidered 'CHU' on the front. My jeans could have used some soap and water very badly. My 'Neike' sneakers were of a comfortable size 9 and half. The baseball cap, with another CHU symbol, had its hood jetting out on the side over my ear. Who ever said I had to have a shave every day?

If I showed up like this for a banquet at the Buckingham Palace, the doorman would have thought I was something that cat brought in on a rainy day and called the trash-collector.

Beaming a big smile, I told her, "Barbara, that string of pearls on that beautiful blue dress makes you look gorgeous".

"Cut it out Rohit. What do you want? What is it this time?" she asked, wasting no time on small talk trivialities.

"How does David's schedule look like this week, Barbara?" I asked, still with that smile broadly pasted on my face.

"I could squeeze you in this afternoon around 4:30. But for no more than 10 minutes. What is it about now?"

"My life in the Academia seems to be coming to a grinding halt. Along with that endangerment of self-survival is looming large. I am kind of wondering, if I should not be thinking of going on for a Doctorate program".

"Doctorate programs are for people seeking Knowledge and Truth, not Sustenance. Do you know the motto of CHU? 'Veritas Liberitat Voss', that is Latin for 'Truth Shall Liberate You'".

"Is that so Barbara? I thought it meant, 'Truthful Fellow gets liberated from his job by his Boss'. The real reason I told you, is strictly between you and me."

Having said that I slowly walked back to my room. My roommate Srinivas had not yet returned. I opened my mailbox. There were the usual junk mail and plenty of bills, credit card statements and the ubiquitous rejection letters to my resumes. Then there was an envelope with my mom's handwriting on top.

There was the usual sentimental stuff of advising me to eat well and take care of health. There was also a picture of a demure young lady called Seema Dhillon, second child of Wing Commander Rajesh Dhillon of Indian Air Force. She was 21 and an under-graduate student at Lady Shriram College in Delhi. They were interested in a marriage proposal.

Seema's older sister Sangeeta was married to a heart surgeon, Dr. Arun Varma, in Seattle, Washington. They were willing to sponsor for a Green Card as well. I shoved that envelope with its contents into my pocket and tried to tidy up my appearance.

I had that interview with Dr. Kennington at 4:30. He had been my advisor through the Master's program. We had developed a good respect for each other. He was not one of those that would make me wash dishes for his wife.

He said, there were a few research projects on which he could use me. He would run the idea by the Committee. Once the funding is finalized, I could come on board. This also meant my Student Visa could be extended until I finished my Ph.D. That was some reprieve on my life.

That night there was a phone call from Dr. Arun Varma. He does not waste any time. Does he? He and wife Sangeetha were passing by Dallas, the following weekend, on their way to Florida on a trip. They would want to come by and meet me. The purpose was obvious. They wanted to check me out and send a confidential report to their folks in Delhi.

I was angry first at this FBI like background checking business, then at the oncoming onslaught without my asking. Even as I was mulling over the whole thing, that night there was also a call from my mom. She insisted that I play host to them and make a good impression.

CHAPTER 4

Wing Commander Rajesh Dhillon had another couple of years for retirement. He had joined the Air Force at the age of 21 fresh from college. His career was going up very rapidly. His being a nephew of Air Marshall Manik Dhillon did not hurt either. He was carefully nurtured and kept away from any combat duty in most of the conflicts.

He was on the committee of experts to evaluate military hardware purchases. He represented the Air Force on the committee to give expert opinion on air-defense systems. In that course he had to make several trips to European capitals including Moscow, visiting vendors in those countries. The purchases involved a few billion dollars worth of contracts spanning a decade.

In the beginning Wing Commander Dhillon did have plenty of moral compunction. There was an instance when he was shaken from it and made to reshape his life's philosophy.

He was at a wayside cafe in Champs Elysee and his colleague on the committee General Uthappa of the Army broached the subject. A Swedish arms dealer who had submitted a bid had contacted him.

Purchases were always made by inviting bids. The bids are all sealed and opened in closed chamber in the presence of the bidders. No changes or negotiations are allowed after that. However, some seasoned dealers can always find ways around it, if only some committee members could be made to give a helping hand.

Some clauses of the bid and technical specifications could be left vague or unmentioned. The committee was well within its rights to ask for clarification. That is just when one bidder can manipulate his bid and outmaneuver his competitor very legally. On the part of the Committee, their conscience was quite clear that they were not hurting their organization in any way since neither the quality of goods nor the price was in any way compromised.

General Uttappa was due to retire in less than a year. He had 3 daughters to marry off and his eldest son still not graduated from the Engineering College. His nest egg was very modest and not much by way of patrimony either.

He sought Wing Commander Dhillon's friendly understanding and cooperation. He needed that extra vital vote on the committee. They could make a cool $ 50,000.00 each safely to be deposited in a confidential account in Liechtenstein. No questions asked and no fingerprints left.

Wing Commander Dhillon was first taken aback. Then he cooled off and asked his colleague for time to think it over. After returning to Delhi, he also mentioned it to his wife Ranjana. Neither could get sleep that night. They were tossing and turning wrestling with the whole plan. It seemed so harmless. It was all a part of the game. Only ones that do not use such opportunities in life were total fools. After all anywhere you look, every one was doing it, are they not? Just do it once, catch a big fish and then give up to retire peacefully.

At the committee meeting that afternoon, General Uttappa made the proposal that further clarifications be sought from the Swedish bidder. Out of the remaining four members, one raised his pencil and went along.

Two other members voted against. They wanted the Swedish bid rejected and the contract awarded to the most complete bid with the best price.

All were looking at Wing Commander Dhillon. There were moments of silence. Slowly but surely, he also raised his sharpened pencil up and voted in favor of the motion by General Uttappa.

There is always a first time for everything. This was the first time for Rajesh Dhillon as well. Next time he went through this with much less afterthought. And soon this became a normal routine. He had become a part of the team. To make it look good, every so often they would award a contract or two to somebody else.

He got a posting as Air Attaché at the Embassy in Washington DC. That was the time when Sangeetha's marriage was arranged. Seema was still in school. Rajesh Dhillon sill had a few more years in the Air Force. He wanted to complete his full term to get all the benefits of retirement. There was also a good chance of his becoming Air Vice-Marshal before finally bidding good bye to the Air Force.

He was glad he was able to find a good son-in-law in Arun Varma, especially with his being well established in the U.S.A. He could now entrust his account in Liechtenstein to safe hands without in any way implicating himself.

The wedding itself was a grand affair. Families and friends from all sides attended. Seema was 15 and had just started developing breasts. After the wedding reception was over, late in the evening, guests were being taken back home. The car was quite full. Seema squeezed herself into the rear seat, somebody clicked the door lock and slammed it shut.

She soon figured out that she was sitting on the lap of her maternal cousin Sanjay, then 17. He had come from Mussourie especially for the wedding. They had been playing, teasing each other and dancing together all evening.

She settled down gazing at the lights and shops that were passing by. The car swerved sharp, she tried to hold her balance by holding Sanjay's arm. Then there came this big jolt on a pothole when she would have hit the roof, had he not put his hand around her waist and held her firm close to his thighs. They both felt cozy and nice like that.

Then there was a long stretch of drive when there was very little light. Others were busy giggling, laughing and exchanging jokes about the happening of the evening. Slowly Sanjay's hands brushed against Seema's upper blouse. She ignored it thinking that it was just an accident. After a while, it was a more deliberate and slow movement. The palm gently rested over her breast. She felt a very strange tingling sensation all over her body, as she had never felt before. Blood was gushing through her temples and she sat just shrinking momentarily. She was confused and did not know how to react. First she wanted to yell out or push his hand away. But then she kept quiet and motionless, as she was embarrassed. Then it felt good. She slowly rested her head on his chest and cuddled. His other hand was gently cupping her other breast by now. He was softly brushing his face on the nape of her neck. She liked that as well.

Soon the car pulled over at Seema's house. She got out and stood waving at the car as it moved away to drop other people at their respective destinations. That night Seema went to bed thinking about him. Next morning Sanjay returned to his school in Mussourie.

What started as an innocent dalliance that night after Sangeetha's wedding, slowly and steadily blossomed into a more serious involvement. Sanjay and Seema kept closely in touch, metaphorically and somewhat physically as well.

Sanjay's dad was the older brother of Ranjana Dhillon. This relationship could no way lead to anywhere like altar and wedding bells. That might have been possible if they had been Muslims or belonging to some other sects. It had to end sooner or later. Both Sanjay and Seema were well aware of that. But theirs was not a concern that took a very long-term view of things. It just felt good for now.

Within a few months of their encounter at the Wedding, Sanjay moved to Delhi to pursue further studies. There was no question of either of them going on dates. They would go to movies and parties, sometimes in groups and sometimes by themselves. In public they had to behave in a very decent but friendly manner, nothing more.

She persuaded her mom to let her learn driving from him. Buddha Jayanti Park is a large garden without too much traffic. It seemed like a natural choice for them to go there on driving lessons. While he would let her drive and show her how to steer, quite naturally his elbow would brush against her inflated blouse. She did not seem to mind that at all.

He became bolder and bolder then on, on their succeeding lessons, as weeks and months rolled by.

He once stopped the car under a tree. It had become dark. Seeing no one in sight, he embraced her and ran his lips all over her face, neck and finally resting on her blouse. She asked him to kiss her on the nipples over the blouse. He did. Then he put his hands over her neck, slowly slipped it into her bra from above and gently slid it over her bare breast. He gently pulled the breast out of the blouse and softly ran his lips over the very tender nipple. She was in ecstasy. He pushed his other hand under her skirt and started stroking his palm over her soft silky thighs. As she remained enthralled in his kiss with eyes closed, he kept moving that hand further above until he encountered her netted panty firmly enclosing her crotch. He tried to push his fingers through the elastic over one upper thigh. At this point she shook herself away from him and asked him to stop it. He did not force himself.

They then adjusted their clothes and started driving back. They were both silent and emotionally at the brink of boiling over.

When she came back home her parents were sitting in the living room watching TV. They greeted her and told her that they had found a very good match for her to marry. He was one Rohit Sharma, with a Master's in Engineering in the U.S.A.

Arun Varma did not turn out to be quite the son-in-law, Rajesh Dhillon had hoped for. Arun being the eldest had the complete responsibility of his parents and two younger siblings. They were all first living together in one large house. After the marriage, Arun and Sangeetha moved into a different house just a couple of blocks away. The parents still held strong control over the family and its finances.

Rajesh Dhillon wished he had a son. He wanted somebody who would take good care of himself and his wife Ranjana into their old age along with the money he had amassed clandestinely. He was now on look out for such a person to marry his second daughter.

Seema just smiled and went into her room. She closed the door behind her, fell on the bed and turned off the lights, even without changing her clothes. She was too emotionally charged and restless. She just wanted to forget everything and fall asleep.

But she couldn't. She tossed and lay on her belly, raised her hands, rested her elbows on the pillow and clasped it tight burying her face into it. Her torso was on the bed rubbing against it. She spread-eagled her legs. Quite involuntarily she started pressing her hips into the mattress churning into it slowly. After a few moments there was an electrifying sensation flying through her spine. She wriggled for a while and cuddled the pillow even more tightly. She had never felt like this before.

She was savoring the sweet feelings of Today and Now. Everything else could wait until tomorrow. After a few moments, she fell asleep and slowly glided into a dreamland.

Next morning at the breakfast table her parents confronted her again about the marriage proposal. All she could muster in response was that she was not yet ready for marriage and wanted to put off marriage for a few more years. She wanted to study Fashion Designing in the U.S. She had also talked to her sister and brother-in-law who agreed to have her with them in Seattle.

Her objections were promptly overruled. Her dad was due to retire in a couple of years and such good matches do not grow on trees in their backyard. Seema was not getting any younger either. If they put off by a few years, she might as well retire from the matrimonial scene as an old maid and spend rest of her life as a spinster wallflower.

She was no way going abroad without being properly married first. She could study all the Fashion Designing as she wants after getting to the U.S. with a husband.

She was demanded to stop having such a long face and finish breakfast before it got too cold. Her dad took the last sip from the coffee cup, folded the newspaper and was off for his day's work. Her pleading with her mom would have been of little consequence. Between the two parents, she always found her mom the harder nut to crack. In any case such major projects were always at the initiative of her mom. Even her dad did not have any veto power.

Thus her fate had been more or less sealed for then. She decided she might as well learn to like what was going to be inevitable. After all Rohit looked quite nice in the picture and life in the United States would always be so much more fun.

CHAPTER 5

I got a call from Dr. Kennington's office followed up by formal letter. I had been accepted as a research scholar toward a Ph.D., program with a reasonable scholarship. They were also willing to give the formal letters for extension of my Visa. All things settled, I could start by the following Fall.

That left me a couple of months of Summer to visit Delhi and attend to the marriage proposal. I made the bookings and called my mom.

After making the necessary phone calls it was decided that we go to the residence of Wing Commander and Mrs. Dhillon, to visit with the family and meet their second daughter Seema Dhillon. It was a Saturday afternoon and a good 45-minute drive to their house at Vasant Vihar. My mom, Mukesh, Nirmala-bhabi and myself set out all decked up. It was a 2-story house with well-manicured lawn in the front with a cement driveway from a well-painted pair of steel gates.

Rajesh Dhillon himself received us at their doorstep with a beaming smile and folded hands. We all marched in one by one, into their living room. It was spacious with well-upholstered sofas and tastefully decorated draperies. There were curios from his various foreign trips. I also noticed a picture of Rajesh Dhillon in the form of a cartoon with the Capitol Dome of Washington DC as a backdrop.

After exchanging pleasantries with Mukesh, Rajesh turned toward me and started darting his questions. He wanted to know all about my activities and prospects at whatever I was doing. Then came the grand finale.

Ranjana Dhillon went up and walked down the stairs with her daughter Seema well adorned in makeup, jewelry and a dark green Kameez with matching Dupatta and Salwar. She slowly walked up to the sofa beside me and sat down. On the bidding of her dad, she made some tea and started serving us one by one. Along with that we were offered some savory to munch on.

We exchanged glances and polite smiles. She seemed just as comely and demure as she was in the picture I had got from my mom. She had nice large brown eyes and very light skin. When she smiled she displayed a perfect row of pearly white teeth. When I first saw her my pulse started racing. Then there was generally an uncomfortable silence from both of us, as the others started interacting with each other.

The whole process was most painful and embarrassing for me. After suffering through it for about an hour, I heaved a sigh of relief when my mom requested their leave. The bidding of good byes lasted another fifteen minutes, before we were finally on our way home.

After some 5 miles of driving in silence, my mom finally tapped me on the shoulder and asked, "Well, what do you think? We don't have all month, you know? We need to let them know by tomorrow".

Mukesh intervened like a fire fighter, saying, "They have to let us know first, if it is okay from their side, is it not? Why this hurry?" That seemed to make sense.

Within half an hour of our returning home, there was a call from Rajesh Dhillon. They were happy to meet all of us and would consider it an honor if we would agree to this marriage. Mukesh answered the phone. He responded saying that I was away visiting the temple with my mom and we will let him know our reaction by the following morning.

I insisted that I needed to meet Seema alone and should take her out by myself a few times before deciding on this issue of a lifetime. That idea seemed outrageous to my mom and Nirmala. Mukesh abstained from voting, a great diplomat that he was.

"One does not do such things in India. What kind of a girl will do that? Would you want to bring such a girl into our family? This is not your America, you know? You can take her out all what you want, after getting married", they yelled at me.

I was quite adamant. After plenty of wrangling and cajoling, Nirmala-bhabi agreed to talk to Ranjana Dhillon. They negotiated and came up with a game plan. Sangeetha and Arun were coming from Seattle, the next day. It was agreed that we could go out as six-some, Sangeetha, Arun & Seema from their side and Mukesh, Nirmala-bhabi and myself on ours. Oh Boy! Were they doing me a great favor by leaving out the parents and rest of the township.

But they wanted to announce a formal engagement by a week from Wednesday. Then the wedding had to take place within a month. Since I was due back in Dallas 3 weeks thereafter, it left barely 2 weeks for honeymoon.

I even heard them mention if honeymoon was all that important and necessary. After all so much work had still to be done, like getting the trousseau ready, sending out invitations and arranging a grand reception etc., etc., not to mention visits to the American Consulate to arrange visa formalities for Seema. It was planned that she follows me first as wife of a student. Later Sangeetha would sponsor us both for a Green Card in the U.S.

Since the whole course had already been charted out between the two ladies, there seemed little, if at all any, room for me to do anything by way of choice or deciding. I thought to myself, if this is what is happening to an adult male like me, what would be the state of Seema, the girl I was destined to marry?

There were the usual debates about the merits and demerits of the way people get married in the West and in India. Arguments were flung at me that after all plenty of arranged marriages turn out to be just fine whereas even after dating and courting 4 out of 5 marriages in the U.S., end up in the divorce court within the first 10 years.

"Look at our parents and us. Didn't we do well?"

I felt like responding 'It is not how long but how good your married life is. There is more to marriage than remaining un-divorced.'. I was in a terrible minority to enter a fight.

High points of the outings were a picnic to a Lake near Faridabad one Sunday morning and a dinner at the rooftop restaurant in Hotel Intercontinental. We also took in a musical concert at Sapru House and some movies. Seema and I were left alone often to interact, when the other 2 couples purposely wandered away at some excuse.

On my part this seemed like as good a deal as any. She was very good looking, no doubt. She had lived in the U.S., when her dad was in Washington DC, even if she was very young at that time. Which means she must be familiar with the life in America, hopefully. With a good educational background, she must find plenty of opportunity to advance in a career if she chose. Her very influential family connections could not hurt either.

More than anything else I was also very very tired of the wild geese I was chasing, trying to bed the girls on the campus, which invariably ended up leaving me most frustrated. I decided not to resist or fight the inevitable that was charging toward me inexorably.

On her side Seema seemed to be generally a reserved and shy person. Besides, her mom was quite domineering and took all the decisions in her life. She had been quite aware of all the details about me even before we met. Her sister and brother-in-law also had filled her in. She did not have too much to ask me on our outings. She seemed reconciled to the whole idea with little opinion. I did not find that very complimentary. Though I did find her going into some kind of a reverie and drowned in thoughts, every so often. I assumed she was thinking of her life as a married woman in a foreign land.

On my return to Dallas, I had to tell Srinivas that he needs to start looking for another place.

I saw in the Student Center Notice Board that there was a Thai student who had finished graduation and was going back home. He was disposing off his belongings. He was asking $500 for a 15 year old Toyota Corolla in 'running condition' with some 180,000 miles on its odometer.

I took a good look at her. She had tattered upholstery. The glass would roll up the window only with some extra efforts, since it had always been kept down. The owner believed cool Texas breeze is so much healthier than air-conditioning. He claimed it gave him a good 25 miles to a gallon of gas. All it needed was a new battery and a couple of better treaded tires in the next 4 months or so. The original color was probably some shade of pinkish-red. Now it had smudges and dirty patches all over with some kinks and dents, making it impossible for its color to be put in any one description.

I negotiated and brought down the price by a hundred dollars. I had some $150 of my own savings and from reselling the textbooks. I borrowed the remaining ransom from Srinivas, promising repayment of $50 per month.

The Thai student carefully counted the cash and put it in his shirt pocket. Then he shook my hands after handing me the keys. I sat in the driver's seat and cranked the engine. After the 3rd attempt there was a big gurgling noise and the engine started. As I stepped on the gas, the car started rolling with some smoke and bursting-of-crackers noise coming from the rear.

First the Thai student's face lit up, as the car was really moving. Then his face became crest fallen. He slowly stroked the body of the car and with a sullen face told me, "Please take good care of her", as if he was parting with his favorite aunt.

"Don't give it a thought. She is in good hands. Send her flowers for Mothers' Day, if you wish", I told him and drove away. I needed a car quite badly. How could I welcome my princess without a steed?

Within about 2 months Seema arrived. She arrived with a check from her dad for $50,000.00 drawn on his Swiss Bank account. It was in her individual name. I did find it somewhat hurtful that they would give a present not including me in it. At my suggestion, she opened an account with that money in her individual name at a bank near the campus.

For Seema it was not an easy adjustment to her new life. Her previous experience of living in the U.S., was of no consequence whatsoever. She had been brought up in a very different life-style, with parents doting on her every need and servants taking care of all the work. Now she had to do everything herself, that included cooking, washing, cleaning the toilet bowl, laundry, and not excluding carrying grocery bags up 2 floors to our apartment on the campus.

The apartment itself was very sparsely furnished on the 2nd floor with no elevators. She had problems with people's attitudes toward her and her incapability to communicate properly with any one, leave alone developing meaningful friendship. It is one thing to know the English language, but quite another to be able to think on the same frequency as the other people you come in contact with.

The climate was a big change. Texas has very severe summer and winter, unlike in India. Living cooped up in an apartment all the time, as your only human contact is away at work most of the time, can by quite daunting. Having to live with a man that was a closed book, notwithstanding his being her husband, is very challenging in itself.

She had absolutely no idea at all about what marriage and its responsibility were all about, even for Indian life-style and standards. She had very few skills of cooking or housekeeping. She had been brought up with the belief that once she gets married she would acquire all those skills at her husband's house anyway. So why trouble her now? Let her have a good time while she can.

All this was such a far cry from all those glamorous scenes she had seen in the Bollywood movies, with heroes and heroines prancing and dancing with duets on their lips in front of big mansions.

At first married life seemed to move quite uneventfully for me. However I did find Seema not showing much by way of feelings or love toward me. Sex became a routine matter and always at my initiative after gaps of several days. It did not quite cross my mind that there could be any other man in her life and thoughts. I kind of assumed, that must be a typical attitude of an Indian girl.

Sangeetha set our papers for a Green Card in motion. Then on, I was constantly and progressively being made aware, subtly and sometimes not so subtly, that I owed them my life, liberty and happiness, because of this.

There would constantly be phone calls at all odd times, from her parents in Delhi or from her sister in Seattle. She was getting directions and instructions on what to do and what not to do. My presence in her life started becoming a non-event.

One weekend Arun and Sangeetha flew down. They shed tears at the abject 'deprivation' to which their girl was being subjected. The three of them went around shopping for everything in my house including a new car for Seema. There were also these catty remarks about how Arun was able to afford so many lavish things and if I would ever be able to do that. It meant little to them that I was still a research scholar living on my scholarship and my self-respect demanded that I don't take help from anybody else.

I tried ignoring their lack of respect bordering on a patronizing attitude toward me. Soon my workload started increasing as well. I was under a lot of pressure to finish my research project before funding would exhaust. Sometimes that meant my being at the Lab almost all night. Even on normal days by the time I came back home, Seema would have eaten and gone to bed, leaving my dinner on the table.

I had not wanted Seema to idle away her time. So I persuaded her to get enrolled into MBA program at the Clarke School of Business at CHU itself. It was all within walking distance in the campus. I thought that way she will have some interests and diversions. That would also expose her to the local Americans and help her get integrated here.

As days and months rolled by, Seema did finish and get her MBA degree. It was not easy for her to find a respectable job in spite of that. It took quite a while before a Real Estate company would take her in as a trainee. That did not enamour her one bit.

Her mom kept reminding us that we should be giving her a grandson soon. That would give her a good reason to come visit us in America, which was one of her life's most prized ambitions. She came and lived with us for a few months before and after, Munni was born. They were all quite disappointed that it was not a boy, to inherit that big fortune. However, they slowly got reconciled to that fact.

Now all the instructions and directions of how to lead our lives came directly and personally from Ranjana breathing down our necks, instead of over the phone, as was happening so far. It almost seemed like I was orbiting on an entirely different planet leaving them to their own world, which accidentally happened to be my house.

On Munni's first birthday Seema's parents sent a check for $ 100,000.00 in Munni's name. We opened a joint bank account for the mother and daughter. My mom and Mukesh sent a new dress and some toys with a friend who was coming from there. It had become very very obvious, especially to Seema's family that they could pull their weight on me and my life with total impunity. I had no counter-weight whatsoever on my side to prevent their total domination of my life.

Within a year, Rajesh Dhillon retired. He and his wife started working on selling their house and coming over to the U.S. for good. Sangeetha had started working on their Visas. He still had some friends in the DC area. He wanted to buy a house and settle down there. But was over ruled by Ranjana. She wanted to stay near her daughters. Since Arun could not be shaken from his post, they decided to make Seattle their family head quarters. Soon they would be manipulating Seema and myself to move there as well.

After Rajesh and Ranjana settled down in Seattle, it became a routine affair for Seema to pack up and go over there every so often. Some times I would not even be aware of her going until after I got home to find a note stuck on the fridge. I was so totally engrossed in my research project that I had no energy or time left to chase these red herrings.

Slowly but surely my Ph.D., doctorate arrived and I heaved a big sigh of relief. The topic of my dissertation happened to be a hot technical problem on which Texas Electronics had poured enormous amounts of capital for research and development. On recommendation from Dr. Kennington they picked me up as soon as I finished and agreed to sponsor for a Green Card on their own as well.

Seema's family started pressing us all to move to Seattle and live with them. This was not an idea that I relished even one bit. It was bad enough living a couple of thousand miles apart. Living in the same house would have me totally trampled under their one toe.

CHAPTER 6

I put the car on Cruise Control and freed my toes to some relaxation. We were going at a comfortable speed and I did not want to take any undue chances. Archana was nicely ensconced in her seat beside me. I thought we had warmed up to each other enough to venture some down to earth conversation.

"If you don't mind could I ask you something?" I said.

"Sure, go ahead".

"How come a person like you is travelling alone like this? I am sure there are plenty of people from your own line of work, media and paparazzi that would be hovering all over you on every step".

"I am shunning all media coverage. I am here for some very personal medical reasons. I had to consult some specialists in Phoenix, Arizona. My visit is known only to my very close relative, my aunt in New Jersey. My shooting schedules are being taken care of by my doubles. So nobody there is even aware that I am here."

"I sure hope you came out with flying colors on your Medical Test", I said without being too intrusive.

"Yes. Thank God. But I still need to make a few more visits. So far everything seems to be going good."

I did not want to pry anymore. All in good time, if and when she feels like it.

There was mild drizzle and I started the windshield wiper. To break the silence I tried turning on the radio but did not succeed in getting any sensible music. We were now entering North Carolina. We stopped by at a wayside gas station to fill gas, wash up and refresh ourselves with a can of Coke.

By about lunchtime we were at Asheville. The rain had stopped. There was a restaurant on top of the hill with a breathtaking view of the mountains and valleys. There were some clouds and the sun was playing hide and seek. I told her that we have some 90 minutes for respite and lunch.

We were seated at a table with just 2 seats, overlooking the valley on the terrace. The table was very elegantly set.

Starched tablecloth and napkins, shiny silver alongside well laid out dishes. There were wineglasses and a little vase with red rose in the middle. As I was perusing the menu, she excused herself to go powdering her nose.

She came back looking radiant. She had absolutely no make up. She had tied her hair up with a scarf and wearing the jeans and top that we had bought the previous day. I did not wish to take my eyes off her but had to, as I could see her feeling embarrassed at my staring her. She just flashed another of those scintillating smiles and started reading the menu.

I did not want to order any alcohol since I was driving but asked her if she would want some wine or anything else. She also did not want to have any drinks. We kept eating with very little conversation. As we were coming close to ordering dessert, I slowly broached the subject of our further plans.

"We should be reaching Raleigh by about 5, in another 3 or 4 hours. I guess you would want to check into a good hotel. I could take care of that. Then you could be contacting your folks and make further arrangements. What do you think?" I told her.

She took a few moments and slowly replied, "What kind of place do you have?"

"Mine is a 2 bedroom apartment in a complex which is quite neat and nice. We have a nice swimming pool, indoor

and outdoor. Then there is a game room. It is near a canal where I like going for a walk or jog some times."
"Would it be too much bother if I stayed with you?"

"No. Not at all. But you know my pad is not exactly a 5-star hotel that you must be used to."

She pealed out laughing. Shaking her head, she said, "Whatever gave you the idea that, that is what I want?"

Well that having been settled, I continued our conversation.

"Do you feel ignored that nobody here recognizes you and fawns on you with all the adulation and admiration like in India? You must miss all that attention and being treated like some kind of royalty."

"Are you kidding? I love this anonymity. I really like that I am being treated like a normal human being and not like some rare artifact or statue in a museum glass case", she said to my surprise.

Once she said that, my defenses also started breaking down. I felt somewhat relieved that I did not have to be too much on guard while talking to or treating her.

Even though she had come down from the pedestal of a movie star, she still was a stunningly beautiful girl.

I find such beautiful girls intimidating by their very looks. It is almost like somebody is threatening me with a dagger and I need to take shelter within myself. I get confused, how to react.

My very first reaction is one of self-rejection. There is no way this divine looking creature will give a chance to a no-good nobody like me. So why bother? Just keep a decent distance avoiding pain, agony and humiliation.

If by any chance she does cross her path with mine and is nice, I go into my next stage.

Since she is used to being pampered and given a lot of attention by every man around her, I tell myself, only way to make an impression on her is to stand out and not behave like other men. Just be cool. Do not push yourself too hard on her.

Then somewhere in one corner of my psyche I have this image of my being a Rhett Butler trying to confront this Scarlett O'Hara. More you ignore her, the more she feels challenged. She would wish to have one more scalp under her belt and go for that unconquered territory, which is I. Once you have fallen for her, like the others, she will go seeking greener pastures.

So I keep expecting her to come chasing me.

This attitude is of course totally asinine. Not every beautiful girl is a nitwit Scarlett. And I am no Rhett either. I have lost many a nice girl this way. Oh God! I could kick myself in the behind for losing so many such great chances.

Take for example Anita Singh.

She was a Sikhni. She had killer looks. She was a stunner by any standards. She was one year junior to me but in the Liberal Arts. While I kept avoiding her, she did come by to me once, flashing her great smile spilling a string of pearls from her lips.

She was selling tickets for a charity show. How could I not have obliged such a divine creature? I bought the ticket. After some uncomfortable silence, not knowing how to carry on a conversation further, I asked her, while a Sikh obviously looks a Sikh, how does one make out if a woman is a Sikhni?

She once again gave one of those laughs that would make Church Bells toll in any man's heart.

"Good question", she said. After a pause, with great panache she continued, "It is easy. If she is devastatingly beautiful, she ought to be Sikhni".

On hearing that my jaw fell. I was looking askance and agape. Before I could find my tongue somewhere in the depths of my throat, I saw her stuffing my rupee notes deep into her blouse and gone like a cool breeze in springtime. I couldn't have agreed with her more, at least this time.

There were zillions of other men kissing the earth she trod upon. There would be no way I had any chance whatsoever. No point in even making an attempt. I gave her very little encouragement. I used to watch her play tennis with

Vineeta Khanna every evening, as I used to go for tennis practice. Every so often the ball would go to the other court and we would flash friendly smiles. But so far there was still no encouragement or follow up from my side.

I went and gave my name for college mixed doubles tournament. Partners were picked by drawing lots. As luck would have it, I got picked as Anita Singh's mixed doubles partner. We cruised through earlier rounds. We would just stick to the business of playing. At most we would shake hands at the end of the match before parting. That shaking of hands was also just a formal brushing of our finger tips.

However in the Finals, we had to confront the top seed Vineeta Khanna partnering Ranvir Baxi. No bookie would have given us a dog's chance. They were both University Team players.

Ranvir was the kind of a guy who would want to touch a girl at slightest possible pretext. All through the match I could see him putting his arms around Vineeta, as if he was trying out some new game plan or strategy. For no reason at all he would go and clap his palm against hers.

Did I have the decency to even give an encouraging pat on my partners back when she faulted or shake her hands when she scored an ace? No sir! If that was not asinine what would be?

It was the deciding set. We were all holding our service games. The score was 4 serving 5. Vineeta was serving from the Deuce court to Anita at 30-30. As luck would have it she double faulted.

At 30-40, she was going to be serving me at Ad court. That was a game-set-and-match point and most crucial for both sides. I saw Ranvir putting his arms around Vineeta in a conference in the middle of their court. I could pretty well guess what their strategy was going to be. Vineeta would serve from the leftmost corner of her court and serve to my backhand in a very wide angle. I would have no other alternative but to return it straight back to her, if I am able to return at all. Just at that moment Ranvir would move to the center of the net and smash my return right down the middle of our court.

It was a pretty decent first serve from Vineeta. It had plenty of spin, what in Cricket would be called Off-break. It pitched on my line and went way away on the backhand side in a very wide angle. It also had plenty of power. I saw Ranvir moving to the center in a flash. I stepped my left foot back a little bit, turned my right shoulder and set the ball going straight down the side line between Ranvir and the post. It had topspin; it landed just on the corner of their base line and went over the side screen. Vineeta ran for her life to salvage the point, but of no avail. With that, all the people in the stands rose in a big applause. The tournament was over.

I could see the ecstasy on the face of Anita Singh. I was the hero of the moment. If I had run up to her and held her close to me in a bear hug planting kisses all over her face, she would not have objected one bit. In fact, that is exactly what she wanted me to do very ardently with quivering lips, flushed face and shivering body.

Did I do that? Oh No. We Rhett Butlers do not do such things! "Frankly My Deah! What a priceless ass I had been!"

After giving away of trophies, there was a little party. We were playing 'Antakshari'. Anita started with the *Sher:*

"Mera Janaza jab nikla,
Yeh nikla, Woh nikla,
Phir Sara Jahan nikla,
Lekin, Woh nahin nikla,
Jiske liye mera dam nikla"

This translates into English something like:

"When my bier was lifted and funeral started,
Just one mourner came out,
Then some more came out,
Slowly the whole neighborhood came out,
And the whole world came out.
Alas! If only that one person would have come out,
For whom my last sigh had come out!"

Was she trying to tell me something? I was just standing there grinning like a fool with cold feet.

That was it. After that Anita Singh flew out of my radar screen forever. Last I heard, she was somewhere on the

West Coast married to a Stanford Professor and was rearing his children.

If you do not roll the dice, your probability of failure is hundred percent. You live through your life with a rotten feeling of not having had the guts even to have tried. That could be worse than having tried and been spurned.

I was driving, while musing all these past thoughts, as miles and miles of highway were rolling away. Archana had reclined her seat and was snoozing.

Around 5:30 in the evening I finally pulled into the covered parking space outside my apartment. It was called "Players Club" apartment complex at Tournament Drive. There were some 10 buildings each with 6 apartments. Mine was at the ground floor. I had leased mine furnished since there was no point in buying or transporting furniture from Dallas, for this temporary stay.

My apartment had 2 bedrooms, each with attached bathroom, a living room and a kitchen. There was a bar island, separating kitchen from the dining area of the living room. It was fully equipped with TV, microwave oven and kitchen range. I had got a telephone connection installed as well.

I opened the door and let her in first. I asked her to feel totally at home and showed her into the 2nd bedroom. I asked her to dig into the dresser and pick up whatever clothes she liked. Seema always had a set of her clothes, shoes etc for her visits.

I suggested ordering pizza for delivery. We could eat and retire early, as we both had had grueling couple of days. I asked her if she had any preference for topping on the pizza. She said, she would eat whatever I would like to have.

There was no message from Seema in response to mine informing of our plane mishap. She was either not there in Dallas or did not care.

After ordering pizza, I grabbed a couple of beers from the fridge and turned on hot water in my bathtub. Removing my shoes, I lay flat on my bed, staring at the ceiling with my brain going blank. I closed my eyes and tried to renew my nerves. I heard some foot steps in the kitchen and then in the other room. After a while I also heard water running into the tub at her bathroom. I doffed off all clothes and slid into the bathtub squeezing the top from a beer bottle. As I started gulping the first draft of beer, it felt really good.

As I was drying my hair, I heard the pizza man knocking on the door. I changed, came back and sat at the middle of the sofa with arms stretched on both sides. It had started getting dark. There was only whatever light was coming from the TV. After some time she went to the fridge, poured herself a glass of wine and came toward the sofa. My arms were still extended on both sides. She sat close to me nestling between my armpits and chest. Her hair was brushing against my cheeks smelling of shampoo. She was again wearing that long T-shirt from Arkansas.

We extended our legs and rested them on the coffee table in front. We had put off getting physical long enough. We both wanted it very much to soothe our shaken emotional and physical condition. Neither of us wanted to resist it any more. It was not sexual per se but a feeling of intimacy and coziness that we sought so badly.

We ate a few slices and finished our drinks. I turned off the TV and just sat like that for a while. In a few minutes, I could see that she had fallen asleep in my arms, like a baby. I lifted her and put her in her bed. Tucked her nicely in her sheets and turned off the lights.

I was sleeping in my bed soundly by 9:00PM.

CHAPTER 7

Early in the morning I felt that she had quietly slipped into my sheets. I turned and put my arms around her. We kissed most passionately for several moments. Then she whispered into my ears, "I know what you want. I want the same too. But please be patient with me. Let us take it slowly, very slowly." We lay cuddling under the sheets like that for quite a while. We wanted our feelings to take over and do whatever came naturally to us. Our reservations and inhibitions were slowly breaking down. Our feelings were thawing. But we did not want to hurry such a surreal and ethereal gliding into the sublime. We wanted to savor it ever so slowly.

I wanted her to stay on and asked how long more could she stay. She wanted to go to New Jersey, take care of her affairs and return in a day. That made sense. I told her, I had to get ready and go to work that day, especially due to the important meeting in the morning. We decided that I would take her to the airport on my way to work. She was going to call her aunt, make sure they would be there to receive her.

On the way to the airport I told her of our Office Outing that was planned for the coming Saturday. It was going to be a Charity Golf Tournament followed by a poolside barbecue party. I asked her if she would be able to join me. She gleefully said that should be great fun, but how was I going to explain her to my colleagues?

"They have not met Seema and I could always say you are my 'cousin' from back home, if they do insist on knowing", I replied. She laughed.

The following day there was a letter from Seema. She had written it from Seatle. Her folks were pressuring her. They were insisting that we move to Seattle and live with them. If that were not acceptable to me, she would have to seek Separation from the Court. She needed my decision as soon as possible. I was outraged. In all this, Seema herself had no brains or guts to take a stand. I knew this coming. But I was not quite sure, it was going to be so soon and in this manner.

I sat down and tried to gain my composure. I had to think of Munni as well. Then I wrote to her a response saying that I could not just throw everything over-board and come over to Seattle. I still had my current contract that I had to fulfill. Besides I needed to find a job in Seattle first, before quitting what I had worked on all my life. So we have to take this slowly. If and when I do find a job in Seattle, I would not mind moving. But for the present, we have to continue like it is now. After printing the letter from the word processor, I kept one copy and stuffed another one into an envelope to mail.

I was quite sure all this reasoning would not get into their hot heads. They were quite sure the whole Universe had to revolve around their ill-gotten wealth.

I left work early on Friday and was at the receiving lounge when the flight from New Jersey arrived. She was one of the early ones to come out of the gangway. Quite involuntarily we were in a very close embrace. Holding hands, we walked up to the baggage area. She had come with a sizable suitcase. Obviously now she was well equipped in all areas.

It was still quite early in the evening, I suggested that we stop by at my usual Grocery store on the way and finish our weekly grocery. After all she wanted to spend time like any other ordinary person, did she not? She needs to know how grocery, laundry and other day to day chores are done in this American Life.

She was very enthusiastic as we were pushing the grocery cart down the aisles. There were several other customers that had their stares fixed on her face, exchanging pleasantries as we passed them. None of them had the foggiest idea, who she was. They were just captivated by her most beautiful looks.

We were stopping at various shelves, as I was trying to explain to her different items and how they could be used. She had been familiar with many of the things from her previous visits to the U.S., but never had to do these things all on her own. We almost had quite a good idea of what we are going to be having for breakfast, lunch and dinner for the whole of the coming week. As we passed by, we also briefly stopped at one shelf and flipped a carton of prophylactics into the cart.

We pulled into the carport of my apartment-complex close to the entrance of my apartment. I opened the trunk of the car and started rolling her suitcase toward my apartment. I let her enter first. She had brought a bottle of wine in a gift bag that she laid on the dining table. As I closed the door behind after getting in, I asked her if she was thirsty and needed anything to drink.

She threw her shoes and other things off one by one. Then clung to me close and said, 'Right now I am all thirsty for you and you alone'.

We rolled over into my bed and covered ourselves with sheets and only the sheets. I have never made love like that even in my imagination. I could not just believe I was really doing all this in reality.

After a while, we needed something to eat for dinner. While all those things we had bought were still in the fridge, neither of us had the patience to even microwave a frozen dinner. Besides we wanted to do something out of the ordinary.

I suggested Chinese. She agreed saying 'Fantastic!' We called a neighborhood restaurant and ordered for pick up within 15 minutes. But of course, we could not go out like the way we were! We wrapped ourselves into just our raincoats and got into the car. The packages were ready at the pick-up drive-in window.

We made some more love and fell asleep in each other's arms. Every so often during the night, I felt her cheek buried on my chest.

As I was still pondering whether or not to get up from bed, next morning, I could get an aroma of fresh brewed coffee. She had got up much earlier and even gone for a jog. She had her white golf shirt, shorts, and sweatband on the forehead and tennis shoes on. There were small drops of sweat running down her eye-browse on to her cheeks. She was gulping a glass of orange juice. A picture of a perfect health-nut.

We were due at the Golf tournament at 10 O' clock. That gave us a good couple of hours to breakfast and get ready. I popped a few toasts in the toaster. What she attempted as an omelet ended up being fairly well made pairs of scrambled eggs. It tasted good, who cared about the shape? They all end up looking the same after you have swallowed them, don't they?

This whole thing was just too good to be true. Only one question kept coming to my mind.

Why me? She must be having any number of men that would do anything to have a time like this with her. This includes men in the U.S., much better off than me. Beauty Queens, Models and Movie Stars have moved from Bollywood to these shores hitched to some very wealthy NRIs, haven't they? By American standards I am not even in the same league as those. Then, why me? What happens next? She will just disappear from my life like it never happened.

I mustered enough courage to ask her this, as we were racing down the Riverside Drive toward the Raleigh Country Club. The flora in the whereabouts of Raleigh is most fascinating. There are thick pine forests and you cannot see more than 10 feet away on the sides of the road. The two-lane highway winds around on hilly terrain and even in the early part of the day it is quite dark due to thick foliage. It gives very cozy and sometimes even eerie feelings.

She started responding to me slowly.

"Yes you are right about other men wanting a piece of my life. But it is one thing to be considered as yet another 'Trophy' and quite another to be treated with sincerity, dignity and self-respect as a person.

"As a matter of fact in many ways the NRIs in this country are even worse than the fellows back home. There are plenty of these *nouveau riche.* All they have is money, no culture, good taste, education or upbringing.

"Or else there are those Ivy League types that are full of rotten attitude and arrogance.

"All these guys get treated shabbily by the local Anglos and that gets reflected on their behavior toward their brethren from back home. Since they cannot take it out on anybody else they do it toward their 'Country Cousins' coming from there. It is not very often that I find someone with kindness, sincerity and honesty like you.

"I am sick and tired of all that meaningless chatter from very shallow fools, whose only brains are hanging between their legs.

"It is not easy being a good actress. Day in and day out, I have to live every possible human emotion like pain, joy, love and shock. For every scene of death I have to really feel like what would it be to die. Most people die only once. I have to do that several times over. I have to feel and live every role that I have to play. On top of all this I have to suffer phony characters all around me in a world of illusions.

"It is so refreshing for me to come out of that transparent bubble and breathe fresh air.

"I come from a very ordinary close knit family. All this glitter and glamour feels good for some time. But afterwards, it starts choking me. I like to come back and find my original little girl from a middle class family. If I clamor for a little bit of real love and honest understanding, is it too much I am asking?

"I realize this may or may not last for ever. But then it is not every day that I have a close shave with death and total indignity. I want to enjoy every bit of what I have now and stop worrying about tomorrow.

"I have asked my folks in Bombay to let me alone for another 10 days. They only have my aunt's contact, if they wish to get in touch with me. I will be contacting her once in a while to see how things are.

"I know what you are thinking. I am not here with you out of just gratefulness. I really and truly love being with you, every moment of it. I will probably cherish it all my life.

"You are married with a child. I do not wish to break up your marriage or jeopardize your family. As a matter of fact I would do all I can to help you as a friend. I am willing to accept you just as you are without making any demands. Can you not give me some small space in your life?"

I listened to her quietly, without interrupting. She made a lot of sense. I was amazed at her intelligence, honesty and perspicacity. She was not just a Barbie Doll. I needed some time to digest all what she said and work on a reaction. I changed the subject to something more mundane.

"Will you please pull my briefcase from the back seat? I have an extra pair of keys to the apartment, that I would like for you to have. Also one more thing, please do not pick up the phone when it rings. Let it go to the answering machine, all the time. You can of course use the phone for making outgoing calls. I am not sure if you like to stay in touch with outside world on Email. If you do, you can also use the PC in my bedroom, any time you feel like." I told her.

"I quite see your point. Thanks for being so understanding". On my part, it sizably bolstered my ego, individuality and self-perspective. My self-respect had been mauled and marauded by Seema and her family in the past few years.

We parked at the Country Club parking lot and walked into the Club-House. Don Wilsner and his wife Pat were already there. After some speech making we started on an 18-hole Golfing spree. We two started off in one cart following Don and Pat in another. We four were one team.

None of us was very good at golfing but the whole environment was just blissful. The whole setting was most picturesque. The Greens were like carpets laid all around. The different colors of foliage and small lakes made it look like a picture post-card. With cool breeze blowing on our faces and such a most beautiful woman on my side, would Heavens be any different?

More than me I could see a total change in her demeanor. It was as if she had suddenly turned into a teen-age schoolgirl. She was laughing and giggling all the time, even at my Poor Jokes. We had some fruit punch and snacks to nibble along on the cart.

We finished the golfing game by about 1:30PM and gathered for some barbecue and beer around the swimming pool. We were invited to get into the water, but we had not brought our swimming attire. She was getting some firsthand experience of Country Music once again. Some of them were dancing on the floor, as we were sucking on some chicken legs smeared with barbecue sauce.

When lunch got over, we walked down to a lonely spot in the garden and spread a large bed sheet that we had brought. The weather was balmy with clear blue skies. We lay under the tree holding hands as cool breeze was brushing past our faces. After about half an hour, we heard our names being called for a tug-of-war competition between two teams. She was holding on to me tight by the waist as I was pulling on the rope.

As we finally bid good byes and got into our cars, it was a little before sunset. We were somewhat exhausted and swarthy with sweat and grime of having stayed outdoors all day. I asked her if she would like to get into the swimming pool and whirlpool at the apartment complex. She said she wanted to very much, but she had not brought her swimming suit with her clothing from home. On a little bit of persuasion, she agreed that we go to a shopping mall on the way and buy one of her size.

We walked into the Ladies section of Sears and started browsing at the different swimming suits hanging from the rack. She picked a few. I looked around and finding no one even bothered, I went into the closet with her as she tried them on. We drew the curtain and she started disrobing.

Huddled so close to her in such a place made it thrilling. After trying out several, we finally picked one that was a flowery two-piece kind. She looked most gorgeous in them. I could see the excitement on her face as she saw me admiring her in that bikini. After charging it at the cashiers, we came back to the car with the package.

As we got out of the car at the Apartment Complex and started going toward our apartment, I saw her jumping and playing hopscotch at the pavement on the way. I was so happy and excited to see her doing that. I was certain she could not have done that, where she lived in Bombay.

At the apartment we changed, picked up a couple of towels, a couple of glasses and chilled bottle of champagne heading toward the poolside. We were shifting between swimming pool and the hot tub whirlpool, back and forth. She would sit across from me in the whirlpool resting her feet on my lap as I slowly rubbed my palm under her feet giving a foot massage.

Once suddenly, as if out of a reverie, she asked me if we could have very personal email addresses with password to exchange private messages, even after she returned to India. I was quite surprised and pleased. I responded with 'Of course'.

When I came back from work on Monday, I found the apartment cleaned and well organized. My desk with all those letters and papers strewn around, was now well and properly stacked. Seema's letter and my response was neatly kept together in my writing pad. She might have read them, I thought. I had nothing to hide from her. It was nice to have a woman at home who cared.

Next few days rolled off with very little outside activities. I would come home from work and take her to my Health Club. There we would do our aerobics and work out a good sweat. We rented bicycles and went cycling through some wooded trails around the neighborhood. She had got quite familiar with my kitchen. Together we would get a fairly decent dinner ready.

She had her booking made on a direct British Airways flight from Raleigh to Gatwick for Sunday morning. After a few hours of stopover she had to take another British Airways flight from Heathrow to Bombay.

We spent the last day taking it very slowly and easy. We just wanted to spend the day basking in the warmth of each other's company and unbridled passion. So we did. We went jogging in the morning. Then played a few sets of tennis. Having worked out a good sweat and appetite, later we soaked in the pool with chilled beer, barbecue and jazz music playing softly. That was enough for us to come back to bed for a siesta in satin sheets.

All great things have to come to an end. This one had to too. We had known that from the beginning. But when the time came for it to happen, it was painful. I would be lying if I told you that it was not. I could see that on her face as well.

We were putting off talking about what was going to be next in our lives with each other. Do we just part and never look back? Or do we give up other commitments in our lives to live together? Neither alternative seemed pleasing or practical. Neither of us wanted to make any demands on the other. Nor bind ourselves with promises or commitments, which we could not have kept. Yet we wanted to stay together longer and longer. It was too emotional to be put in words.

Finally we did agree on some things. We would not demand anything from each other by way of giving up any other relationships or commitments. Wherever we are and in whatever condition, we would accept each other, staying in touch. There was no name or label to our relationship. Neither of us needs to give apologies or explanations to any one. We would under all circumstances meet at least once in a year on this day to celebrate the anniversary of our new lives.

I was pulling her luggage on its roller with one hand and holding her hand with the other. She checked in at the counter.

Before going through the gate, she turned and came back running. We clung to each other as tight as we could. As the sound system started blaring 'last and final call for boarding', we slowly and reluctantly released each other.

After a few minutes, all I could see was a shiny aluminum blurb slowly vanishing up into the skies. My Dream had put on wings. And it flew away into the clouds.

CHAPTER 8

The previous week had just flown past like a dream. I still could not believe it had really happened. The whole of Monday was taken by meetings and phone calls.

When I came home there was another letter from Seema in response to mine. They insisted that I come down to Seattle first and then start looking for a job from there. They were quite tired of my delaying tactics. It was now or never. They wanted to know my decision before the end of the month, before they approach an attorney. That was enough aggravation for me to take a few things and throw on the wall. I kept the letter in rest of the pile. I will think about it later.

The workweek was very hectic as the day approached for finalization of the project. I wanted keep myself totally drowned in work so I don't have to think about my personal life's two contrary forces pulling me in different directions.

As I came to work on Tuesday morning, I got a call from Don Wilsner 's secretary. Don wanted me for a one on one meeting. When your boss calls you for a meeting suddenly like this, it is either a good or bad news. I had no foreboding, as to what this one was going to be.

We started off by commenting on the weather and how badly the Dallas Cowboys had done in Monday Night Football. Having cleared this routine, I was impatient to get down to the real purpose of this encounter.

I felt like yelling at him, "Spill it out Don. How are you going to call firing me? 'Strategic Restructuring' or 'Corporate Policy Redefinition' or some other nonsense straight from Harvard Business School? Everybody knows how to cover his own bottom before taking care of Corporate Bottom Line. I am sure you have done yours too. All this applies only to menials like me. Whatever you call it, Firing is a Firing. Shoot!"

However I kept quiet, letting him broach the subject. After all it was on his behest that we were having this meeting. He flicked a few imaginary specks of dust from his coat lapel. Then he slowly pulled out his spectacles and even more slowly pulled out a white handkerchief from his trouser pocket. Then with great care started polishing the glasses. All this was a sure sign of dark clouds coming down with thunder and downpour, a proverbial 'calm before the storm'. Then he started to speak.

The upper management had told him that the Company was acquiring a new power plant near Bombay, India. With that there would be a need for somebody to organize their data-processing division there. He could think of nobody that he could trust more than me, at this distance. He wanted to know if I would consider taking that job. I would be stationed in Raleigh. I would still be reporting to him. That entailed frequent travelling between Raleigh and Bombay. It also meant I would have to move from Dallas to here. He said I could take as much time as I needed to think it over and also to consult with Seema.

I was quite taken aback and overwhelmed. It was such an anti-climax to what I had marshaled all my defenses for. I shook his hands, thanked him with a big grin and came back to my seat. It was too much too quick for me to digest.

A week later, I got a call from a Northern Electronics in Seattle. Their management team was scouring for a new Manager to head their Research and Development division. Research Triangle Park near here was a hub of hi-tech industry. There were several candidates from there that they were interested in interviewing. Instead of flying them all to Seattle, their panel had planned an Interviewing Center in Raleigh for candidates in and around this area, They had heard about me and wanted to know if I would be interested in that position.

Within the next 5 days their panel arrived in Raleigh and we had a daylong interview at the Hilton. Theirs was a company in existence for about 5 years and the current head of the R&D division was due to retire in a couple of months. They had some very ambitious expansion plans with fresh finances being pumped into the company from abroad. I would be located in Seattle with some light travel nationally and internationally.

After the interview was over, I thought I had done pretty well for myself. They promised to review all the candidates and let me know of their choice in the middle of the following week. This seemed like a pretty good chance for me to put my family life back together.

I took my flight to Dallas that weekend. Since Seema was still in Seattle, I took the airport Shuttle Service to get home from the airport. There was a big pile of mail on the floor, dropped through the mail slot. I collected them all into a plastic trash bag. I would sort them out later into good, bad, junk and super-junk categories.

I tapped on the telephone answering machine to retrieve messages.

I was surprised to hear a voice calling himself Sanjay. He had called from Portland, Oregon, the day I had left for Raleigh. He was pleading with Seema to come and meet him at Seattle. It seemed to me from his talk that he had been calling and talking to Seema for several months now. But this time she had forgotten to erase the message.

Then there was still my unretrieved message informing that I had escaped being killed in that fatal air-crash.

I took my flight from Dallas to Raleigh on Sunday as usual. There was the Wall Street Journal in the pouch in front of me. Just to keep myself engaged, I pulled it out and started browsing. There was one news item that caught my attention.

It was about Northern Electronics of Seattle. It said there was an unknown film personality from Bombay, India who had shown keen interest on buying majority stock holding in this company. With infusion of such large capital, this company was predicted by the financial analysts to do extremely well. It continued further, by saying that this Investor made the financing conditional to the company restructuring its R&D division by hiring a younger and more energetic manager. However there was no mention of who this 'film personality' Investor might be. I could only make a very well educated guess.

After a couple of days, I got another phone call from the CEO of Northern Electronics of Seattle. Their Board had approved my appointment. They wanted me to come aboard, as soon as I could get away from the present contract. They wanted to know my joining date.

I wanted to sleep over the whole matter. There were too many decisions and choices to be made. Each one would have far reaching effects. Each course of action would lead my further life in an entirely different direction.

It was obvious to me that Archana had read my correspondence with Seema while rearranging my room. She realized that she could help save my marriage by arranging a job in Seattle. But I loathed this whole idea of others manipulating my life and taking any help from this Benefactor from Bombay. I did not like the idea of going to Seattle even otherwise, especially after knowing what Seema had been up to.

I called Northern Electronics and told them I was unable to accept their offer and move to Seattle.

Next morning I called Don and told him I was willing to take him on his offer. That was by far the best choice I could have made from both personal and career objectives. This was a job that I had got on my own merits. I could still keep my ego and self-respect intact in every way. In terms of the two ladies in my life, I could look at my face in the mirror next morning not feeling rotten about myself.

I came to my apartment from work. I wrote to Seema saying that I had accepted this new job offer in Raleigh and it is entirely up to her if she wishes to get a Separation from the Court. I further told her, if she did, I was sure to fight for Munni's custody. It was plain to me that she had written that ultimatum under the tutoring of her mother. My defiance might have surprised her parents. But with whatever little brains or guts she had, Seema would not have expected or wanted me moving to Seattle. But that was a choice they had made. Ball was now in their court.

Having changed into my swimming trunks, I headed to the swimming pool and dove into that crystal clear cool water. It gave my head much needed cooling off.

Before turning in that night, I checked my Email. There was an electronic Thank You card, signed 'yours Archana'.

THE END

COMING TO AMERICA

On the 9th of October 1977 I departed New Delhi for moving to the United States. On the 13th of October 2000, I completed 23 years since arriving here.

My stint at spending some months in Europe a few years earlier made my transition to the 'American Way' of life somewhat less of a 'Culture Shock'. Still quite a few things seemed strange.

My host at that time watching a Baseball game on the TV told me with great excitement, that it was the 'World Series' going on, expecting me to share that ecstasy. That was a game being played between a Club in one part of the country with another Club a few hundred miles away. I told myself if that is your "World", I must be an alien from outer galaxy! This month, 'World Series' is being played between 2 Clubs in same city called 'New York City'. If 'Shivaji Park Cricket Club' should play the 'Bombay Gymkhana', would you call it the World Cup?

But such questions don't occur to me any more. 23 years have taken their toll on softening my attitude.

I had some adjusting to do before I got used to the American way of calling people. In the British way that we are taught in India, everybody is either your superior or inferior so need to be called by Surname with a Mr. or Mrs. or Miss as a prefix.

Here everybody is called by his or her first name by default preferably by the nickname. Even your boss will call you by your nickname, put his arm around your shoulders with a grin, before firing you and saying 'it is nothing personal, just a downsizing in our effort to please the Wall Street'. He may even ask you for some leads for his own job hunting efforts if I had found one for myself.

That was a far cry from the Gestapo techniques of German companies I had worked for before coming here.

It also took me some time to get used to the etiquette, lingo, spellings, pronunciations and expressions. I had to unlearn quite a bit of my Indo-British ways and relearn the new way, consciously or sub-consciously. It is quite possible I might have fallen somewhere in between making this Trapeze jump.

Take for example those words that have special connotations, American style. A 'guy' does not necessarily mean a male *homo-sapien*. It could be female or even a material or abstract entity. Then 'bitching' does not mean a female canine that trades carnal pleasure for monetary gain.

It is a behavior that is preponderantly stubborn, unreasonable, bad tempered and nasty as displayed by any person of either gender or a thing.

I wondered why do I have to smile and say hello (preferably by name) whenever I cross somebody on the street or hallways even when I don't know that person from Adam? Now that comes to me quite involuntarily.

Then there are of course the unmentionable bathroom manners of using toilet bowl and toilet paper! The light switches work differently here. You push them up instead of down when you want to turn anything on. The traffic moves on the 'wrong' side of the road. People still measure in miles, pounds and Fahrenheit. These are of course minor trivialities.

I still don't feel quite comfortable wearing baseball cap in reverse gear or sneakers with my trousers.

When I watched the American Football, I had a hard time figuring out why in the heck so many fellows were fighting with each other at different parts of the field when the ball was at quite a different spot altogether? It takes a winning home team to turn you into a fan of the game. I am now a fan of the Dallas Cowboys, even though they have not done much of winning in the last couple of Seasons. The Stars and the Mavericks follow closely.

My first job was as an Encyclopedia Salesman at a cold and dry West Texas little town called Odessa. I was walking down a neighborhood with my African-American (you are not supposed to say 'Black'), boss. A cop pulled us up and asked for our IDs.

I found that quite unpalatable in the "Land of the Free"! The ID had to be something credible like a Driver's License.

Later my partner explained to me that it was a kind of 'crime prevention' effort! People in that neighborhood did not want some bums loitering without purpose.

I quickly learnt that to be counted as a person, you had to have a Driver's License—even if you do not drive a car.

That job did not last very long since they wanted me to sustain myself on a commission and not a fixed salary. The next 18 months were like doing hard labor at a prison camp. I worked in a sweatshop at a wage of $1.10/hr. I could not be paid less since that was the minimum wage by law. Only two persons in that place spoke English and were legally allowed to work in the country, one was I and the other was the President of the company. I picked up a few sentences of Spanish from my 'undocumented' Mexican co-workers. One of which is 'Mucho travacho, pokito Dinero' meaning, 'too much work but too little money'.

When they found out that I could read, write and count 10, they gave me the responsibility of Inventorying meat packages. At the end of the day when the stocks did not tally, my Supervisor told the President that I did not know how to count, while in actuality it was he that was stealing the stuff, giving to the women working for him in exchange of 'special favors'.

Whenever I asked my Supervisor for a raise, he would give me more hours of work at the same rate per hour. I was still able to balance my monthly budget and save $700 to buy a 10-year old Toyota Corolla, which had some 100,000 miles on its odometer. All cash down. I had no idea why would people want to borrow money or have things called 'credit cards'. I had been brought up with the credo that if I had the money; I could buy, if not go without it. I asked my neighbor to drive me to the Drivers License Department before I could take a Drivers test. I paid 45 cents per gallon of gas.

Only in August 1979 I found a desk job and I moved to Dallas. I drove some 350 miles of dusty Texas road in my Toyota without A/C; windows rolled down and wind blowing through my hair, one Saturday afternoon for the job interview. Raj Kapoor could not have done it better on a camel back, singing *"Mera Joota Hai Japani..."*. I had all my Bachelor's and Master's degrees besides testimonials from 15 years of career, tucked under my armpit. My prospective employer asked me just one question. 'Do you know how to type?' I said 'Yes'. I got hired.

Dallas had one Indian restaurant. After finding about it in the Sunday newspaper, I drove several miles to hunt it out. They would serve *Masala Dosa* every Sunday morning. In all there were about a 1000 Indian families in a radius of about 50 miles. Once in a while there would be some performance of an Indian artist on a tour of the country. But

Dallas was always an 'also ran' town where they would come only on a mid-week evening, on their way to some other Big City that got the 'prime-time of the week' spots like Saturday evenings.

As I would drive on LBJ Freeway, I would wonder why in the heck they would want to have 3 lanes on both sides when there were hardly a handful of cars driving in either direction.

It is amazing how things have changed now. Indian restaurants and grocery stores are mushrooming all over town. We have an 'Udipi Café' and a couple of restaurants serving authentic South Indian *Shappadu*, on plantain leaf.

Being a center for Electronics and Software Industry besides having several schools and universities, you cannot pass a day without bumping into some Indian anywhere you go.

We have a movie theatre that just shows Indian movies on 5 screens everyday—in Hindi and regional languages as well.

No month passes without any of this bigwig Show-people showing up with a blockbuster 'Live-in-concerts'. Aishwarya Rai, Shahrukh Khan, Karishma Kapoor, Aamir Khan, Akshay Khanna, Shushmita Sen, you name it. They have all been in Dallas within the last one-year. These events get so crowded and expensive, it is much better to stay home and watch them on TV. That is back to Square One.

Like any normal Indian boy, I grew up developing a passion for cricket. Even as a pre-teenager, I used to bowl and bat on the dusty street in front of our house. When we could not get a real cricket ball, my friends and I used to play with tennis ball and any wooden stick for a bat. As I went to College I almost made it to my college team as an opening batsman and off-spin bowler. Some months ago here, my Pakistani neighbor who was another cricket maniac and I got into an argument with an American about the merits and demerits of cricket versus baseball. As you can imagine that was not a debate any one could go home with a win-win situation.

I used to miss cricket so very much after coming here. But only cricket I could get was the one chirping in my fireplace!

I have now 5 channels of Indian programming on my TV via satellite dish. Ajay Jadeja has been hosting a program called 'Cricketer of the Millennium' which I have been following keenly. He narrates and shows clips of some very fascinating personalities and events that I remember so well from past, when I used to follow the game with ears glued to the radio. CKNaidu, the 3 Vijays - Merchant, Hazare & Manjrekar. How can I forget that rainy English summer when Vinoo Mankad retrieved some of Indian pride at the Lord's in 1952 after Alec Bedser and Freddie Truman gave the purge of 0 for 4 wickets at the Leeds? Or Eknath Solkar making that magnificent catch to get Wadekar and his team a victory at the Oval in 1970. Of course that new found 'Wunderkind' Gavaskar on the Caribbean tour of 1971.

We now have at least 5 different teams playing cricket in the Dallas/Fort Worth area.

When you slice the trunk of an old tree across, you will see different layers of fringes of its bark, from its different stages of growth, the innermost being the oldest from its stage as a sapling. Human personality is very similar to that. Layers of different influences keep piling up on one's psyche. I spent first 37 years of my life in India, in its different parts, that have had their influences on my personality. The next 23 years in the U.S. have their experiences overlaying that. But the influences at childhood and formative years are so much more powerful—one year of the childhood is not same as one year of adulthood.

How much Indian and how much 'American' am I? I don't know.

I can still wear a dhoti, sit on the floor and swipe *Rasamshadam* running all over the plantain leaf. Then I also enjoy a cold mug of beer and a well-broiled Texas steak. I am still a Hindu and have delved quite deep into its beliefs, history, philosophy and theology. I understand the sentiments of performing *Shraddham* or *Sandhyavandanam*. But if I had not worked in a beef-packing factory, I would have starved to death. Wouldn't my forefather Aryans that wandered the slopes of Himalayas chanting *Rigveda*, agree? They were hunting and gathering for surviving, is it not?

Not everybody has same experiences or has to make same choices. Life is one long road strewn with conflicts to be resolved and compromises to be made. When I visit India I find many Indians trying to be more Americanized then I and be proud of it, while I try to be my original Indian self, expecting them to treat me as such.

I come across numerous Indians here that try to insulate themselves into their own little cocoons trying to prevent outside winds of change blowing into their faces. Sooner or later one has to make a choice—how much blending of 2 cultures is palatable? Even when we were growing up in northern or western parts of India, we were trying to preserve our Tamilian traditions as we knew it at home, while the Tamilian culture in the South was getting evolved differently.

I was in Thailand some time ago. They took me about a 100 miles from Bangkok to show their old capital city. It is called 'Ayuthiya' built by King Rama the IIIrd in the 18th Century AD. I wondered if BJP should not build Babri Masjid here and make everybody happy.

There are people of Indian origin in Fiji, Guyana, Bali and several other places where they practice Hinduism as they brought and transplanted a few centuries ago. In many ways, their brand of Hinduism is more authentic than one in their homeland today. But then, the Good Lord had not yet created MTV and Internet at that time.

Today Dallas/Fort Worth Metropolitan Complex (Metroplex for short) has grown far beyond I could have imagined when I first came here. LBJ Freeway is so congested at peak time that bumper to bumper traffic extends as far as eye could see. This gargantuan Leviathan is gobbling all neighboring little towns up into satellite suburbs.

When I went for the interview to get the U.S. Citizenship, I was tested whether I had workable knowledge of English and Civics. The English part was easy enough. Then when the interviewer asked me questions on Civics it was interesting.

By the way, I have a Master's degree in Political Science from India. I had to study the Indian Constitution and its history in great details. I also had to study 5 other major political systems of the world namely British, American, Swiss, Soviet, Chinese and French. The Indian constitution itself is based on the British Parliamentary system and the American Federal system. Therefore I was very complacent and confident of facing the Civics questions of the interview.

First she asked me to name the 2 Senators from Texas. I could muster the name of only one. She grinned and said that was fair enough.

Then she asked me what were the first 10 amendments to the American Constitution called. I pondered for a while and said, 'I guess they are called the First Ten Amendments'. Eureka, how could I go wrong on that?

She laughed and said, 'Smart, but there is a special name for that, what is it? Do you know?'

I was bowled over. I had not got the foggiest idea. I pleaded ignorance.

She laughed again and said, 'Shame on you. That is called the 'Bill of Rights''.

I was thinking in terms of the Indian Constitution. 'Bill of Rights' is known in the Indian Constitution as the 'Fundamental Rights'. That is the very first provision of the constitution.

"How could that be called an amendment? If that itself was an amendment what would be the constitution prior that?" I asked her.

She laughed again and said she did not have the foggiest idea. She passed me on the test anyway.

On the day I was sworn in as a U.S. citizen, I had mixed feelings. At the pit of my stomach I somehow felt I was betraying my country of birth. I am sure I was not the only person in that large hall feeling that way. There was this lady from the Immigration Service who gave us a very nice and soothing speech before we took our oaths. It may sound like a cliché but true. She said we should not think like we are losing a country but as gaining one.

The U.S. allows dual citizenship. According to the U.S. Laws, once having acquired U.S. citizenship you may not regain it if you decide to renounce it.

At that time India did not allow dual citizenship. Lately there has been a lot of talk of India allowing dual citizenship as well.

This weekend I am going to cast my vote in the Elections. Who am I going to vote for the President? Ralph Nader sounds very good. But nobody will vote for him because nobody else will vote for him! Would I? Probably not. Then who do I prefer between Tweedle Dum and Tweedle Dee? Definitely not the one YOU think I am certain to vote for. When it is all over I can always pat the guy who wins on the back and say 'you're my kind'a guy'. Everybody loves a Winner. Don't we all? Did you vote for Richard Nixon or PVNarasimha Rao? Nixon is a 4-letter plus 1 word, PV who? Do we know them?

In all these 23 years I have come a long way, literally and metaphorically. I have all the clap-traps by which people measure a person's success. I have earned Master's Degrees. From minimum wage my annual income has grown to a 6-figure number. I own a 3-bedroom villa on a 1-acre lot on the shores of Lake Lewisville. I drive a BMW. Like all this really matters.

I have membership to Country Club and access to some very upscale social circles, nationally and internationally. I have friends from all national, ethnic and religious backgrounds, from both genders and all walks of life. I have visited the national capital and socially met Senators, Congressmen and officials of the Administration on one to one bases. They all have treated me with utmost friendliness and courtesy, heeding to my political, social and economic concerns.

I really feel I have integrated well into the fabric of my adopted country.

Now when I meet new entrants from outside especially India, I see in them the same enigma of attitudes as I had 23 years ago.

America as seen through the windows of Hollywood movies, glossy magazine pages and TV shows besides the ideological rhetoric of politicians, is quite different from what you see and feel when you come in contact with it in reality.

A country is not in the skyscrapers, steel bridges, flashy cars, and highways with neon signs. It is in the flesh and blood of its people. To know the country you must know the people and speak their language. Knowing the language is not just to learn the vocabulary and grammar. It is being able to think like them. For that you need to get this whole thing called 'culture' into your psyche.

I also still own an apartment in New Delhi. For the past 5 years I have been visiting India once a year. I stay constantly in touch with my family and friends there. This has become especially easy with the advent of electronic communication. I run a monthly newsletter website on the Internet to keep all my family strewn across the Globe in touch. We are in constant touch on the e-mail.

In my thinking and attitude, I am quite a queer combination of Indian and American cultures. I love them both.

When I travel outside, whether nationally or internationally and come back here, I truly feel I am coming back home.

I just try to be myself, as honest and truthful as I can muster to be and get away with. Twenty-three years is a long time. It is all still fresh in my memory. I have some very unpleasant and some very good experience. So it is in this whole world. Is it not?

THE END

SOJOURN

(All incidents mentioned in this narration are real. So are the characters. Do not try to look up these names in Telephone Directories. They are either not alive or you have only their first names here)

As my flight was approaching to land at the New Delhi International Airport, my thoughts were wandering back to my childhood in a sweet little town Udaipur in the state of Rajasthan.

PART 1

We lived in a villa on the banks of the Swaroop Sagar Lake, a villa that was the official residence of the Prime Minister of the local Kingdom before the princely monarchies were constitutionally abolished. The villa was several miles away from the main town and Sohan Singh our Chauffeur would drive me to and fro school.

While driving back from school, he would let me sit by his side and steer the car, my legs would not reach the pedals on the floor. He would roll down the window on his side and take a few puffs. We had a perfect quid pro quo, I would tell nobody that he took puffs in the car in front of me and he would let me steer the car. Sooner or later my legs started growing and reaching the pedals. I even got my own driver's license.

That was a sad day for Sohan Singh, his puffing privileges were severely curtailed then on. In fact if Sohan Singh had his way, I would not have got my license for another few years. He disapproved of the way I negotiated curves. My acceleration and deceleration would curdle the blood of his 'driving guru'. If I kept shifting gears like that, the valves and cylinders of the car would be ruined in no time. As for parallel parking, I still got it all wrong by at least 10 Degrees! But luck would have it otherwise. One day, while my mom was having a heated debate with Mrs. Sahi on a matter of earth shattering consequence, whether or not an extra dash of turmeric was really needed in the recipe they both had got from the Commissioner's wife at the Field Club, I oiled my way talking Uncle Sahi, the District Superintendent of Police into agreeing getting me the license.

Next day promptly an 'Orderly' rang our front door bell in his starched uniform, bearing in one hand, the results of Mrs. Sahi's attempt at putting the recipe in a tangible tongue tingling form and an envelope of my Driver's License in the other. Puff your lungs out Sohan Singh, now on I am on my own with the second car!

The school itself was in the middle of a farm. If you looked out of the classroom window you could tell the season by the crop growing around you. Whenever we had a free period, we kids would run and sit by the well. Two blindfolded bulls would go round and round in circles drawing water from the well with a Persian Wheel and spilling it over a mud canal. I would spot a twig and follow it on the flowing water, recalling each of its stopping places with the ports of Marco Polo our teacher had just told us in the geography class. We could run into the fields and pick up fresh carrots or maize (corn?) to be roasted on charcoal, eaten with lime and salt or a stick of sugar cane to be squeezed into fresh juice. I tried so hard to make a mango out of wet mud ball, bake it and paint it for my class project; it would look anything but a mango. We would wait for the bell to ring on the final day of our Annual exam some time in April or May. We would hand over the answer sheets to the teacher and race out of the school like we were prisoners just reprieved by the President. Summer holidays!

Oh how we longed for it from September on. Until the results were announced and grades came out, we could pretend as if we were the best students in the whole district and have fun without a care in the world. During the sizzling summer days one could barely head out during the day. Come evening, our retinue of servants would sprinkle water on the terrace and put rows of cots and beds out in the open for the whole family to sleep. With cool breeze blowing from Swaroop Sagar lake my dad would show us all the different planets and galaxies in clear blue skies; or before turning off the lights, he would read from Oliver Wendell Holmes, Dickens, Alexander Dumas or Jane Austen. Then there were the Uncles, Aunts and cousins from both branches of the genealogical tree, not to mention our own nieces and nephews.

That was my idea of having 'quality time' with an 'extended family'. Dr. Richard Austin of Houston, a psychiatrist of sorts that Judge Robertson appointed, in my child visitation trial recently was explaining the idea of 'extended family' to me. To him it meant ex-wives with their ex-husbands getting together trying hard not to fly at each other's throat and pull each other's hair for the sakes of their half and step children. My aunt would a fold paper several times and cut a figure from it, when she unfolded it there would be a bunch of figures all holding hands with each other, like Dr Austin's 'ex-' tended family of copulating couples. He even charged me a fortune to explain how it worked.

During Winter Holidays after I graduated from High School, my mom arranged for me to spend the vacation with my uncle Annaji in New Delhi. That was my first visit alone outside home and first visit to the Capital. New Delhi was still very much like Lutyens had designed and built for the British. Only the White Big Brass was replaced by Brown Big Brass, my uncle being one of them. He had a bungalow on 13 Roberts Road.

Heck knows who this Roberts was, probably some English army man with walrus moustache, solar hat and khakis, that showed exemplary valor in the jungles of Burma (when no one was watching), laid his impotent boss's horny wife, got this act of bravery mentioned in the dispatches 'back home'. The new nationalist government would not have any of that nonsense. They promptly renamed the street as *Teen Murti Marg*, meaning the street with 3 statues!

That change of name got a very safe passage through the Security Council of the United Nations. John Foster Dulles and Andrey Vyshinsky agreed on one thing after a very long time. The Arabs thought that it did not go far enough to denounce the Balfour Declaration, but was a good beginning. David Ben Gurion chuckled and ducked the issue, after all India was a signatory to the declaration creating Israel. Chiang-kai-Shek loudly applauded the move trying to win some friends in the newly emerging countries. The French sought further clarification. They wanted to know if one of the 3 statues was of Monsieur Dupleix. They were told that the 3 statues were those of the Unknown Indian Soldiers from the 3 Services. However there was a street close by that still retained the name of Monsieur Dupleix. They were not totally satisfied, they feared, what was the guarantee that some other Nationalist may not change that name also? Despite not being given any such assurance, the French finally decided to go along, quite reluctantly. Sir Anthony Eden maintained a stiff upper lip and directed the British Ambassador to the U.N., to abstain from voting.

At the end of it all they all clinked champagne glasses toasting for World Peace, patted each other on the back and went home.

The Defense Minister lived 2 houses down the road, and the very legendary Prime Minister Jawaharlal Nehru lived across the street. Our house had large sprawling lawns in the front and the back with red gravel driveway. Blooming bougainvillea adorning the front porch. Connaught Place, the main shopping area had elite shop windows where one would only gaze at the mannequins and not dare ask the prices. One could still buy imported liquors and perfumes if you could pay for them. You could dress very well and go strolling around in the evening and ogle at all the other well dressed women and girls. There was the Volga restaurant where you could have a rendezvous with the elite and peer out of the window at the flashing imported cars and neon signs. Any place farther than 8 or 10 miles from this place was oblivion.

Back in Udaipur, what we thought would last forever, came to a sudden end one spring afternoon. 16 hours workdays without respite took its toll. The ticker could take it no more. Pulling a corporation from its morass into an undertaking of viability and respect had its price to pay. My dad suffered a heart attack while working in his office and collapsed. Our attempts to revive him with CPR were of no avail.

Nearly half of the town or so it seemed, showed up for the funeral. People had the belief that being a pallbearer insured their own path to the 'Hereafter' safer. They would vie with each other for a chance. It took me several days even to let the facts of what had happened seep into my thoughts.

The Banyan Tree had fallen and we suddenly found ourselves exposed to the whirlwinds of the real world. All this while we had been sheltered by him and had been very comfortable under his shadow. There was always the 'Dad knows best' attitude and complacency. Wherever we were or whatever we did, at the back of our mind we always felt we could fall back upon him to bale us out of any situation. Now there was a big vacuum and void that could not be filled.

After the mourning period was over, the towns people decided to name a locality in the city as 'Dore Nagar', in memory of my dad. I left Udaipur for Bombay, looking for a job in the City of Opportunities.

PART 2

Well my next visit to New Delhi was when my Managing Director of the German Company in Bombay, told me that there was too much sales talent concentrated in Bombay and he wanted me go take over the department in the New Delhi office. I had just arrived after a year's stay in Germany and going around Europe, which is supposed to give one a 'Perspective', not an 'Attitude'.

I had lived in Bombay for 5 years prior to that and had got used to its pace and demeanor. Bombay is to New Delhi as New York City is to Washington DC. Tall buildings, stock-exchange, lots of money, before shaking hands each tries to find out how much money can he squeeze out of the other's palm. In contrast, one needs to know the Mechanics of how the shortest distance between two bureaucratic tables is not a straight line in this City of labyrinthine cobbled streets;

you may think you have a lot of political clout and leverage because your second cousin is a Member of Parliament, little knowing that your rival's wife screws the Cabinet Minister himself and volunteers for his Fund Raising Committee (sure enough she raises 'fun' for him and later his brats of indeterminable paternity).

I met Anil at the Volga restaurant for coffee. I had known Anil for a few years in Bombay. We had last parted company about a year ago at a party there. Anil was going to UC Berkeley for a PhD in Structural Engineering. I was leaving for training in Germany. Girls had no hard time choosing between us. The good old U.S. of A was any day a greater bargain than a refurbished and retreaded Europe, what if he had a few extra pounds at the midriff? They all wanted him. However both of us returned to India.

Connaught Place was still the center of action. Shop windows only displayed stuff made within the country. Gone were the flashy imported cars replaced by locally made ones; there were only 3 such models, though you had plenty of colors to choose from, unlike Model-T. There were also those ubiquitous auto-rickshaws and scooters alongside buses packed like a can of sardines spewing smoke like the Vesuvius. The outskirts of the city extended up to about 20 miles from Connaught Place (CP as it was affectionately called). Sidewalks did not have that smartly clad sauntering anglicized persona of elegance; there were those bunches of unwashed, un-scrubbed seekers of Nirvana on their way to Nepal, with odor that would send any police dog haywire.

My one bedroom apartment or flat was about 10 miles from CP where my office was located. It was in the southern suburb of Green Park. South Delhi had the neighborhoods of people with discriminating tastes. Jor Bagh, Defence Colony and Chanakyapuri were out of the question; you could only live there if you were married to the daughter of Indian Ambassador to Brussels (or she would marry you only if you were one of those living there). Rest of New Delhi was very bourgeois. You could know all about micro and macro economic theories of class struggle between have's and have-even-more's at parties where you could be invited only if you belonged to the Inner Circle. Young men dressed in Levi's jeans at the bottom and Indian colored Kurta at the top, with beard, smoking Havanas and holding a small peg of Chivas Regal on the rocks, would fling all the cliches and jargons. When cornered by sheer logic, they would immediately take shelter in a line, something like, 'what do you know, I got it all at Harvard or Yale'. Oxford and Cambridge were passe. London School of Economics still made the grade, just barely. Splitting the infinitive? May be, okay. When the music would start playing the Beatles or the Beegees, they would make a beeline to their equally well informed female counterparts, to try out the latest hip steps.

I bought a 20-year-old Ford Zephyr for four thousand Rupees, from somebody who had been transferred out of town and was desperate to get rid of it. If I had done some background checking and known just how desperate he was, I could have brought down the price by half. It got the nickname of Old Faithful. Its color was an indescribable dirty green. She never let me down even though on some cold winter days she needed some extra persuasion to start early in the morning. It would take me a good 35 minutes to get to work. Getting into the flow of things, I had a house warming party at my apartment while my landlord was staying with his expectant daughter on the floor below. Instead of just warming the house, I found I had got it to a boiling point. We were doing the shrug/frug to the full blasting sounds from my stereo of 'Let's Forget Domani'. Sure enough Domani never came, instead came my landlord a minute before midnight. His daughter did not believe in induced labor. Would we keep the decibel level down or make arrangements to move elsewhere. In exactly a minute later he pulled the fuse off our mains. I gave it a serious thought and decided to move to a more salubrious neighborhood.

Within walking distance from 'CP', I found a one room rental with a large terrace; in Manhattan it would be called a Penthouse, in simple Delhi lingo it is called Barsati, a room where people run for shelter if it starts raining in the middle of the night while sleeping on the terrace. My landlady was Mrs. Thukral staying on the ground floor. Between her and me there was one more floor having a cute friendly family. Jan was from Cologne and worked as a journalist at West German Embassy, his wife Afsal was from Hyderabad, with a Master's in Social Sciences, taught in a school for the handicapped children, they had a little son Kai and a little girl Laila. This buffer between my landlady and my stereo sound should work out pretty well, I figured. I gave Mrs. Thukral all the deposits and advance rents she wanted and moved in.

Anil found a satisfactory job even though the salary was nowhere near what he could have got if he went back to America. I was getting settled in my job as well booking some nice juicy contracts from the Indian Railways. We developed a good size circle of friends of both genders. The term Yuppee had not yet been coined, but we were just that. After a party at my new apartment, my cousin Suguna told me that Ena liked Anil and if he would ask she would gladly go out with him. I passed this subtle message faithfully. Before you could spell Gunga Din, I got the news that they were engaged to be married.

Udaipur was within my sales territory and I decided to make a pleasure cum business visit there. Sohan Singh came with a car to meet me at the airport. He had extra gray on the eyebrows and moustache alongside more lines of wrinkles on the sun baked cheeks. But he had the same proud eyes and almost paternal smile. I thought he would ask me if I ever got that parallel parking right. Instead he said they wanted me to come and lay a corner stone for a children's park in Dore Nagar. Udaipur not only had an airport now but an extra railway station, a radio station and several industries. You did not have to go elsewhere looking for livelihood; you got it all here itself with the smoke and squalor as trimmings. Sohan Singh had with him his oldest son Devi Singh that worked in Zavar Mining Company. I gave them all a good hug. I reminded Devi Singh that he still owed me 5 marbles for beating him in a game of Gulli-danda. He smiled avoiding eye contact and said 'of course'; meaning how could I argue with my master's son, leave alone beat him in any game. They asked me, is it true that in big cities like Delhi they had big radios that showed cinema you could watch sitting in your own living room?

New Delhi had 2 TV channels. One was boring and the other more so. The government in its own sanctimonious self righteous perception wanted to make TV not a medium for entertainment of urban elite but for social change especially of the rural masses. But the TV station was located in Delhi with a transmission radius of 30 miles within which the only mass rural or otherwise was that of the deadbeat politicians. Once a week there would be re-run of 15 year old Hindi movie and once a month a re-run of 30 year old Hollywood movie, just to keep the thinking man on the streets of Delhi interested.

One day I parked by 13 Teen Murti Marg and tried to take a peep into the gates. The Sentry told me that a Big Brown Big Brass lived there now. Ordinary Brown Big Brasses were so many in number that they had to be housed in high rise apartment complexes 20 miles away and transported by buses! Annaji had retired long since and was living with his son in Lucknow. He had chronic intestinal ailment. I asked him to come to New Delhi and look up some better doctors. After some pulling of political strings, he was admitted to the All India Institute of Medical Sciences, the foremost research institution in the country. He went into a coma. Every now and then he would come out of it and talk. That man had a memory that would make a super-computer wilt. Even in that state he could recall facts like he had it all in a compact disk drive between his temples. His CPU could put a Pentium processor to utter shame. All the test results showed no conclusive results on what ailed him. My mom was in town and I took her to visit him. She was just 1 day older to him and they had both been through a lot together. She bent and gave him a peck on the forehead. That was very touching. As you grow older and see your contemporaries leaving one by one, you feel lonely and forlorn wondering when will it be your turn. It was all over one day, as he started vomiting blood and never came back to consciousness. His body was brought to my apartment for some religious ceremonies before being taken to the cremation grounds.

New Delhi was the oasis for my business principals travelling from Germany to Canton Fair or Hong Kong or Tokyo. They would stop over for a jet lag respite. Of course it did not hurt to go to Agra and take a picture in front of the Taj Mahal, you could put it all on your expense report anyway. End of November saw a swarm of these business travelers passing by here. Being the local representative of their business, I would keep them generally pleased. Even though it was not in my job description, doing a good work in this area helped a lot to further my career, like perfecting one's golf swing while working for IBM. When my company car was not available, I would use my Old Faithful. Oberoi Intercontinental was brand-new and the only five-star hotel of international standards. They would all stay there in rooms on the upper floors overlooking green golf course with spick and span carpeted hallways whispering elevator music. They would drink Western wines, eat Western cuisine, hear Western music and talk how Western culture had bettered the lot of the world. They would of course have a picture of themselves taken in front of the Taj Mahal to show their friends back home that they 'did India' in 2 days. One of them once took me aside and whispered, "Do you know? Taj Mahal was not built by Indians at all. It was built by Italians". I said, "Yes of course, everybody knows that. It was built by the fully owned Italian subsidiary of Nippon Construction Co., of Osaka, Japan".

They all had standard questions for which I had standard responses.

Question: "There are so many starving Indians and so many starving cows, why don't one eat the other and be happy?"

Response: "Because cows are very gentle and refuse to eat men and be happy".

Question: "What about your caste system? We in industrialized, democratic, free, 1st world countries have classless society of equal people".

Response: "I could say the same thing, but not with such a straight face. If you really believe that, buy my Old Faithful, she runs on colorless odorless free bovine excreta".

I was taken aside and told, "That fellow is the son-in-law of the Chairman of the Board, ear marked to inherit the Industrial Empire one day and you should not have been such a smart ass with him". I said, "I rest my case on classless society".

However I must add this person with whom I had that smart chat became my very good friend and even now after nearly 30 years we exchange Holiday Greeting cards.

PART 3

The stewardess gently awakened me. She said we are going to be landing in New Delhi International Airport shortly and I should buckle my seat belts keeping the seat upright. I was shaken from my reverie back to reality. Here I was coming to New Delhi from Dallas, Texas after an absence of more than a couple of decades.

Passing through Customs and Immigration was extremely smooth. This was the first time I was coming to India on a U.S. passport. I had to get a visa to enter the country. My emotions were too mixed up to grapple embarrassment. My brother had come to meet me at the airport with an air-conditioned car. He let me use one room in his flat that he had got air-conditioned. He found on his last visit to

129

Washington DC that people in America wanted everything air-conditioned.

I had booked a rental car with Budget. After settling down, we got to their office and got the rental car. For $5 extra per day, I could also get a chauffeur. Having watched the Delhi traffic coming from the airport, I grabbed that deal. The car was of course air-conditioned. In India traffic is supposed to go on the left side of the read, one more inheritance of British individuality. But in reality one drives on either side. It is also survival of the fittest philosophy, you go left or right or sometimes up and down as well. Lanes are marked on the road but that is just a formality.

Anil now worked for the World Bank in Washington DC. He and Ena had a girl Shibani and a boy Akil. Anil gave me the whereabouts of another mutual friend Surendra. I gave Surendra a call and we decided to meet for coffee at Volga. CP looked so different. It had multi-storied skyscrapers all over the place. I was told the periphery of New Delhi extended beyond 30 miles spilling over neighboring states. The stores in CP carried foreign brand names like Reebok, Neike, Izod, Pepsi, Coke, Doritos, but all made in India. There were a few more brands of cars locally made than before. Parking spaces by the street side were at least 2 or 3 deep. Volga served some good Indian Kingfisher beer. I stopped converting prices from rupees to dollars, and just gave a handful of Rupee notes to the waiter and asked him to keep the change.

Mrs. Thukral at 60 Babar Road got a surprise of her life to see me. We started ticking off common memories and people. Kai was in Delhi married to an Indian girl. Laila was having two kids and living with her English husband in New York City. The trees on the street had not been felled but half a mile away there were fly over highways and 30 story commercial buildings. Come 5 O'clock in the evening, they all spilled out zillions of working men and women trying to get back home. Mrs. Thukral smiled and said her apartment is never without well paying tenants. Who knows, next time I see her she would have pulled down the 3 story house and put up a 30 story apartment complex, on top there may be a true Penthouse with a skyline for a view, not just a Barsati. We all get Americanized sooner or later. Who was I to preach her?

Progress (?) and jobs have a price to pay. The whole city was belching smoke and dust like it was one big incinerator gone out of control. Windows of the car were always rolled up with A/C in full blast. I was not sure if Delhi had got changed or my perspective had changed after living in free wide spaces of Texas so long. I guess both are true. I get that kind of claustrophobic feeling also when I go to New York City, Boston or Chicago. I asked Puri my rental chauffeur to take me South Delhi. While there was one Ring Road before there were two now. Ring Road is equivalent of American Beltway circling the city. South Delhi still had the better neighborhoods. It was still not the most elite. There were also other very livable residential districts. There were several more 5 star hotels like Hyatt, Sheraton and what have you. In comparison, Oberoi Intercontinental seemed drab and dreary from outside.

We decided to take a weekend trip outside Delhi. To breathe some fresh air and also have fun. We found Bharatpur Game Sanctuary was within driving distance and on our way back we could visit Fatehpur-Sikri and Agra. It took as about 2 hours just to get past outer fringes of the City on a Saturday early morning. Later we drove through some small hamlets and I could see little children with their backpacks zealously going to schools, even though it was a Saturday. There were signs of pharmacies and doctors' clinics. All that seemed very comforting to me. Out on the countryside they had had good rains and there was greenery as far as eyes could see. Roads had strings of large trucks carrying I do not know what, some things some people needed somewhere very badly, I am sure. Puri had to stop the car and was told we could not go further because the road was submerged in flooding rainwater. But then came another and told us that he had a tractor, which could carry us and our car across, for 'a small fee' of course. I was glad free enterprise system was catching on. We finally made it through.

Bharatpur is in the state of Rajasthan and just like Udaipur, used to be a small Kingdom before being merged into the mainstream democratic India. Its jungles, lakes and marshes made a perfect habitat for migratory birds. Birds come from Siberia looking for warmer climate in winter to hibernate or breed. You could find countless species of birds and animals here. It used to be a happy hunting ground for hunters including Imperial dignitaries from time immemorial. They have erected a stone plaque with names of yet more Army Officers with walrus moustache, solar hats and khakis alongside counts of birds they bagged.

Talking about these plunderers, there was one such fellow that was the Governor of Madras in day's bygone. When he finally returned to England, he purloined one large cache of gold, diamonds, pearls, rubies and such other trinkets that would put the Borgias to shame. Poor fellow before he kicked the big bucket, he got pangs of bad conscience, found religion and decided to donate a part of the booty to start a school for destitute children across the Atlantic. Anybody heard of Yale University?

However the government declared this area as a sanctuary for birds and wild life, a few years ago. You may shoot these creatures only with a camera.

We checked into a Tourist Bungalow outside the gates of the Sanctuary. For a very reasonable price we could get a good 2-bedroom suite with A/C and a color TV. We were not allowed to drive inside the Sanctuary. They had cycle-rickshaws. It is a tri-cycle with a seat that can take 2 people. A man pulls from his seat in the front by pedaling. The cycle rickshaw drivers here also doubled as guides. They were trained to explain everything that was going on there in 4 languages: English, German, French and Italian. I told him I would much prefer if spoke to me in simple Hindi. We spent the whole of the afternoon going round in this unspoiled piece of picturesque paradise, so different from the hustle and bustle of the previous days. My cycle rickshaw driver would every now and then burst out with a chuckle at some of my wisecracks, showing glimmering white teeth between dark unkempt beard. I wondered if he ever had ulcers worrying about interest rates or Dow Jones or mortgage payments. Why would he, he was sure he was going to get a good square meal this evening. Tomorrow is another day.

Next morning we headed toward Fatehpur-Sikri. Here I need to pause and take you back a few centuries.

American Republic is a little over 2 Centuries old. India has seen rise and fall of at least 4 or 5 such civilizations in recorded history. Most recently was the Mughal period that lasted from mid 16th century for about 200 years. Babar the founder of this dynasty was a progeny of the great Chengez Khan of Mongolia and a follower of Islam.

He was driven away from his homeland. He came toward India looking for a good place to build an empire. Since he saw no Realtors that were willing to make him a deal, he put together an army and said this is a mugging, out with your stuff.

Till then the Kings on the Indian side thought they had the latest state-of-the-art war machinery like spears, bows, arrows, shields, elephants and horses. They had cut back on Defense spending.

Babar had something called gunpowder that could blast cannons out on long trajectories. The Indian side had a good 100,000 strong brave soldiers, 5 times that on the other side, but were in a total disarray when these cannons started landing on their tents.

The Home team had to surrender to the Visitors before the end of second quarter; Super Bowl was over before the half time.

There had been several invasions in the past through the Hindu Kush ranges on the border with Afghanistan. But most of them would just loot, maraud, kill, rape and go back with the booty. This fellow Babar was pretty serious about his empire building idea. He settled down and said this is my home now on. Immigration & Naturalization Service could not declare him as an undocumented illegal immigrant and deport him. After all he had better guns. Rest is history.

Babar's grandson was Akbar the Great. Akbar inherited the throne when he was 8. At 16 he found his Regent very incompetent, corrupt and unpopular. The Regent was given the good old pink slip. Akbar took over the reins himself. His reign lasted nearly 70 years and the empire extended from the borders of Persia to Burma and almost till the tip of the Indian peninsula to the south.

How he was able to keep together a territory of this size speaks about his management genius. The only other contemporary empires in the world of comparable magnitude were Czarist Russia and China. They had not yet coined the term Super Power. Western Europe was still in bits and pieces. Shakespeare had been born. Apple had not yet fallen on the nose of Isaac Newton.

Akbar was getting old but his wives could not give him an heir to the throne, which worried him very much. There was a holy man in Fatehpur-Sikri about 100 miles from Delhi who had a reputation of having mythical powers. So the mighty Emperor came to this holy man seeking divine intervention to his dilemma.

Sure enough Queen Jodhabai conceived a child and gave birth to Prince Salim. Akbar was so impressed that he decided to move the capital of his empire from Delhi to Fatehpur-Sikri. I am always very wary of these super-natural phenomena.

Whenever I was grounded in my room to do history homework, I would gaze at the picture of this Salim. As I doodled on his face, I always thought he had a strong facial resemblance to the Imperial Chief Harem Keeper, especially the nose and lower chin. In matters of State and National Security one does not argue with the mystical powers of holy men. I would draw a moustache and a small goatee beard on Salim's face so nobody else sees the similarity. In those days nobody knew of Invitro- or Artificial Fertilization. Who knows what went on behind those veils of Royal Chambers?

Fatehpur-Sikri has all the monuments built during that time still intact. When asked how come these buildings are so well built, one gets a wise crack that in those days they did not have contractors with lowest bids, they had an Emperor with a mighty whip.

On one building they show symbols of Hinduism, Christianity, Islam and also the Star of David. Akbar tried to keep harmony between his peoples of different faiths. He even founded a new religion combining all of them.

They also show Roman and Greek influences on the columns of some buildings.

Prince Salim called himself Emperor Jehangir when he inherited the empire. It was easy enough for holy men to live in Fatehpur-Sikri, but it was soon found that for housing a capital city of a large empire one needed large quantities of water supply. Fatehpur-Sikri had very little. Jehangir moved his capital back to brand new quarters in Delhi. He still had fond links to the erstwhile hometown where his very birth was 'conceived' biologically and metaphorically.

Taj Mahal is in Agra about 15 miles from Fatehpur-Sikri. Jahangir's son was Shahjehan who was madly in love with his Empress. She died before she was 30 years old while giving birth to a child. Shahjehan promised her that no one could ever take her place in his life and asked her if she had any wish that he could fulfill. She said that she wanted a monument of their love be built that would symbolize it for eternity. Thus came about *Taj Mahal*, the mausoleum where this Empress was laid to rest.

For a long time I procrastinated a visit to *Taj Mahal*, while I lived in New Delhi. I thought it is just another of those 'images' that Travel Magazines promote and dumb tourists flock to get themselves photographed with. I visited it for the first time when some outside guests had to be accompanied.

When I saw it in reality, I was totally consumed by its sheer beauty. It is out of this world. Its perfection is breathtaking. Made completely of white marble and located on the banks of Yamuna River this piece of art makes one just stand there aghast if not turn to tears at its magnificence. It has inspired writers, painters, artists, poets, musicians, novelists and lately moviemakers. Lovers from all corners of the world, whether in their teens or in their golden age, come here and take a vow. A kiss here under the Full Moon is considered divine. Folklore abounds on its theme.

It seems there used to be a receptacle in the dome where rainwater would accumulate and all the time a drop would intermittently fall on the grave of the Empress, symbolic of her lover's tears.

Now that is very poetic and romantic, right? If that should happen in my living room, it would be called a leak, symbolic of my tears at high Property Tax.

Shahjahan had wanted to build a Black *Taj Mahal* across the river for himself to be buried. It would stand out in Eternity saying 'She was pure as driven snow and I am still grieving for her'.

Destiny had it differently. Youngest of Shahjahan's four sons, called Aurangzeb speared a Coup d'Etat. He killed his 3 older brothers. Took pity on his dad and took him a life prisoner, instead of beheading. Announced himself as the Emperor. Shahjehan asked only one extra favor of his son, that he be imprisoned in a cell wherefrom he could watch his *Taj Mahal* until the dying day. The wish was granted. After death he was also buried in the *Taj Mahal* beside his beloved wife.

Little is known about the architect and artist that designed and built *Taj Mahal*. In those days there were no Copy Right or Patent laws. One way in which an Imperial Potentate could ensure that no one else replicates his creation of splendor would have been to send its creator to learn play ice hockey in 'Gulag'. What was this 'Michelangelo' or 'Vinci' that created this marvel like? There seems so little on record.

Depending on whom you ask, Aurangzeb was driven by either religious conviction or blind bigotry. He believed that the country had strayed from the path prescribed in the Scriptures. The 'Tax and Spend Liberals' had run the country too long, wasting federal funds on wanton pursuits. He disapproved of freedoms to Infidels in their wayward 'Life Styles'. That had bad influence on the good followers of the Path. He wanted to put an end to all that. Music of any kind was bad morals and Arts were degenerate. Paintings show that he had long white beard. He prayed 8 times a day, led a frugal personal life and forced strict moral behavior by his standards on the people.

Aurangzeb might have been very strict and stern with his subjects. But at the domestic front, he had a problem. His dad had set bad precedent. His own Empress wanted a *Taj Mahal* for herself.

She felt belittled. Her friends at the bridge table and cocktail circuit must have teased her.

"What kind of a husband are you any way? Can you not make me a simple *Taj Mahal*? Am I any worse than my mother-in-law?" she must have yelled at him at the breakfast table, in her curlers.

Aurangzeb relented and let her have one. This one is some 1200 miles south-west of Delhi near Bombay. I have seen both, the original and the second version. Comparing the two is like comparing Champagne with Root Beer. I guess Aurangzeb and his wife got what they deserved.

With advent of Aurangzeb started 'The Decline and Fall of Mughal Empire'. The Empire started breaking down. There were revolts everywhere. The Europeans who had come as traders became mercenary soldiers taking sides and inciting quarrels amongst the several factions. One whole civilization came down to the pits.

We headed back home Sunday evening. On the way we were talking about how some new industries that were creating jobs in the surrounding area were also causing pollution to tarnish the white marble of the Taj. I suggested that probably some Walt Disney should take over the whole town and turn it into a new theme park. That would create a lot of jobs too.

I spent the next few days lazing around at home watching TV. Now cable TV in color was available with more than a dozen channels. Even in regular channels the program were very watchable. You had 'Good Morning India', on the lines of 'Good Morning America', there was a Hindi version of 'Wheel of Fortune', one could also see CNN, Talk Shows, Game Shows and Hindi MTV/VH1. There were live broadcasts of Republican National Convention from San Diego, BBC News and Movie Channels. ESPN showed sports of Indian and International interests. You had them all.

Wanderlust took over again and this time I went on my own with my driver to a more serene place called Kumaon Hills. This is an area in the foothills of the Himalayas, nestled in woods, with lakes, water falls, log cabins, hunting lodges, all covered in fog and floating clouds, with sun shining through now and then. I spent time contemplating sunset, sunrise, fresh drop of dew on the petals of blooming chrysanthemums and such other creations of art, that I usually have no time to do in workaday life. I tried to preserve the idyllic beauty of these. I zoomed my lens and kept cranking my camera like I wanted to carry every nook and cranny of this place back with me.

There is a National Park here called Jim Corbett Park. Who was this Jim Corbett? Yet another in 'walrus moustache, solar hat and khakis that bilked native nabobs in dice game or plundered palaces and mausoleums of precious jewelry to be shipped back home?'

No Sir. He was a solid chap, a folk hero. That is what he was. He knew the terrain of Kumaon like the back of his palm, better than his back-yard in Shropshire, Yorkshire, Brookshire or any other 'shire he came from in the Blity.

I could think of him as a Lone Ranger riding along the hills and valleys of Kumaon. When confronted by a big wild cat, Jim would look straight into his eyes and tip the hat. In return the beast would curtsy him and they would wander off in their different directions. Jim would do the same with local humans. 'Mutual Respect' was the key word that pervaded when he was around. He believed in treating the Wild Life and the Humans with an even hand.

Though there was a section of tiger population that would disagree with that.

They are called man-eaters. They believed that Jim was definitely slanted toward the humans.

Tigers like politicians start off as pretty decent fellows. As they go through the rough and tumble of life, some of them may be thrown to a corner and forced to make hard choices.

Like whether to die of starvation or eat human flesh. Instincts of self-survival would generally override. Once they taste human flesh and blood, like politicians tasting intoxication of power, they get hooked on to it. There is no turning back. Gourmet food is what they want always; rest of the stuff is bland meat. They would not settle for hamburgers and French-fries any more.

That is when Mr. Jim Corbett would step in and cry foul. He would get his shotgun or whatever he could grab and go after these renegade erstwhile friends. He bagged a couple of dozen of these in his lifetime and also wrote very interesting books about these escapades. The scourge to human population was brought under control.

But after Jim Corbett vanished into eternity, poachers and hunters (of human species) abounded. Local taxidermists made record profits. Movie stars and celebrities vied with each other wanting to wear skins that would bring the 'Animal' out of their men folk. Tiger population started to dwindle. Tigers had to be declared as endangered species.

The benign apparition of Jim Corbett still pervades on the Hills of Kumaon in the form of this National Park. It is a game sanctuary where all these wild life are protected. Again, you may only shoot them with your camera.

You may drive around with windows of your car rolled up. Remember these lands belong to those members on a different rung of the Evolution Ladder. You are an intruder. There is a road sign that clearly says 'Leopards have a right of way'. So if you find them climbing on top of your car's hood and making faces at you through the windshield, it is their prerogative.

Do not call the Highway Patrol. These are the Highway Patrol.

However you have a better alternative. You can whistle and hail an elephant. Unlike your car they have a trunk in the front, you may not be able to load your travel bags in it though. But sure you can let it siphon a lot of water and give you a fine shower. After you climb on top of it you can generally take a supercilious and condescending view of the rest of the world. At some 25ft above the ground you are also quite safe from rest of the wild life. Breathe fresh air and wander around the whole place for as long as your bottoms can take the bumps.

When I tried to get into Jim Corbett Park, I saw a "Do Not Disturb" sign at the entrance. Tigers were busy propagating and preserving their species. It was breeding time and they do not like voyeurs. The Park was closed for the season.

I had to catch a plane back for London. So I came back to the real world from Shangri-La. My brother asked me if I did not want to go visit Udaipur.

For a fleeting moment it seemed pointless. I had heard that one person I needed to impress most and make proud of my parallel parking skills had been taken away by upper respiratory ailment.

I told my brother, 'May be next time'. I still had to recover those five marbles for winning in the game of *Gulli-danda*.

Airlines announced my flight was ready for boarding. I headed to the gates. For the flight to Texas was beckoning me.

THE END

POTSHOTS AT HOTSHOTS

Southern Methodist University, Dallas, Texas, conducts Distinguished Lecture Series where people that have achieved distinction in their field are asked to share their wisdom with the general public. Between 1986 and 1992, I became an avid participant of these Lecture Series. There used to be about 4 to 6 such lectures in a year. At the end of each lecture, the audience was allowed to ask questions of the Lecturer. I rarely missed an opportunity of jumping from my seat and running up to the microphone and throw a question. A thrilling experience at getting 5 minutes of fame! As a front seat ticket holder (that did not come very cheap), I also got to hobnob with the Distinguished Lecturer at a small reception at the end of the evening. Getting heady and intoxicated by rubbing shoulders and pumping hands with the mighty and powerful over some punch and cookies, was an educational experience.

Following are some of the questions that I asked along with the responses that I got. While the questions are reproduced verbatim, the responses are paraphrased as what each said in 'essence and effect'. You may not always agree with some of the 'tongue in the cheek' responses, but the exchange of words would definitely provoke some thoughts. You may even come out with some of your own views and reactions to these questions. If so please do not keep them to yourselves and share with your friends.

Dr. Christian Barnard (Surgeon from South Africa that performed the first heart transplant).

Question: As technology to transplant organ progresses, it is conceivable that all organs of a person could have been transplanted including brain cells. Then what would it be that would make that person still himself or herself?

Response: We will not transplant human mind.

Edwin Newman (NBC News).

Question: If you were a nominee for the Supreme Court, how would you balance the values of Individual Liberty on the one hand and needs of National Security on the other?

Response: Very carefully, of course.

Charlton Heston (Hollywood Actor).

Question: Do you have any political ambitions?

Response: A good politician needs to be a good Communicator and Motivator. That is why an actor can be a good politician as well. I have been approached by both the parties to run for Congress.

Sam Donaldson (ABC News).

Question: It took a small nondescript newspaper in Iran to break the story of Iran-Contra deal. How come the multi-million dollar newsmen not excluding yourself could not do it? How many such scandals are going unreported as we are speaking now?

Response: I wish I could have laid my hands on the story first.

Dr. Robert Ballard (Maker of the underwater Robot that explored the 'Titanic')

Question: Do you see a parallel between the 'Titanic' and the 'Challenger' disasters?

Response: Yes. In both the cases people were a little over confidant about their technology's infallibility.

Edward Heath (Former British Prime Minister).

Question: Civilizations seem to rise and fall in cycles. Do you think Europe has reached its plateau and will slowly start declining as a cradle of civilization in the coming decades?

Response: No. European Civilization will revive itself.

Elli Wiesel (Holocaust survivor and Nobel Peace Laureate)

Question: In this age of a possible Nuclear Holocaust, do you believe the instinct of self preservation will prevail over the instinct of self-destruction, in human species?

Response: Even though it may seem that the people in power have their priorities all lopsided, we have survived so far have we not?

Caspar Weinberger (Former Defense Secretary)

Question: What is 'State Sponsored Terrorism' and which state does not sponsor terrorism?

Response: It depends upon who does it and doing it in a way that it cannot to be found out.

Tom Brokaw (NBC News)

Question: TV and Radio networks are basically in the business of peddling popcorn and Pepsodent. If they also provide news, it is only as a means to that end. Why should one not doubt your objectivity?

Response: We are not influenced by our Sponsors.

Robert MacNeil (MacNeil/Lehrer News Hour)

Question: If one needs to listen to standard Queen's English, one would probably listen to the BBC. How would you compare that with the standard of English spoken on the American TV and Radio?

Response: Who speaks Standard English? We conducted a survey and found that most people even in Britain did not speak that way anymore.

Robert Bork (Nominee for Supreme Court that could not get Confirmation from the Senate).

Question: There seems to be some controversy over your role in the Nixon White House when he fired the Watergate Independent Prosecutor. Would you like to comment on that?

Response: I was just following orders. If I had not done it some one else would have. Things would have happened just the way they happened regardless of what I did. My only mistake was not having immediately called a news conference and told the public about what I was made to do.

Dr. Henry Kissinger (Politician of repute)

Question: You have had an admirable life but there is something about it that is enigmatic. You know the pain and suffering under the Third Reich and Gestapo from your own childhood. But when you were in a position of power and influence you collaborated with some of the most brutal and suppressive regimes in the world. How do you explain that?

Response: What regimes?

Question: Iran, Pakistan, Bangladesh, Philippines, Argentina and Chile?

Response: The United States is not the Policeman of the World. We have to do what is in the best National Interest and we cannot tell our Allies how to run their countries.

Alistair Cooke (Masterpiece Theater on PBS)

Question: Your talk about American Humorists was most interesting. But you left out my favorite Humorist, P.G. Wodehouse. How come?

Response: P.G. Wodehouse was not American.

David Brinkley (This Week on ABC)

Question: You newsmen report on other public figures. But after all you are yourselves products of the same system and capable of similar behavior. Who reports on your conduct?

Response: Our lives are an open book.

THE END

TRYST WITH A MYSTERY WOMAN

INTRODUCTION

Hindu society is patriarchic. Ancestral worship has been practiced in several societies and at several times in Human history. In the Hindu society it is practiced even today and is taken very seriously, especially in the Brahmin community of the Southern India. A ritual called 'Shraddham', is performed that offers prayers and food to the departed ancestors. It is the ardent wish of millions that they have a male progeny that would perform this ritual for them when they have died.

On a lighter vein, while we proudly trace our ancestry to several generations, can I be totally sure there had never been any outside intrusions in our supposed lineage? Also, just as I invite my ancestors to my house for food and prayers, how about if the role should be reversed and I go back in time and visit them?

I was looking at the Genealogical Tree of my Family. Then I started wondering what would it be like to meet the lady 6 rungs above my generation. A good portion of my genetic makeup comes from her, right?

Is it not such an accidental quirk that I am what I am and that I am here at all? What if that Lady there, or for that matter any body in between her and me had made a different choice of mates? Would I still be there as I am now?

Read this fictional journey back in Time and Space through the Genealogical Tree of my family.

I was travelling from Bangalore to Madras. We were driving down this hilly dusty road as night began to fall and all of a sudden there was a thunderstorm. It started pouring like one big dam must have burst overhead. There was lightening and thunder.

As we approached a curve, the car gurgled a few times and came to halt beside a large Banyan tree. Driver Murugan got out of the car. He opened the front hood holding an umbrella over his head. After peering into the car a little while he came back. I rolled down the glass to hear what he had to say. The carburetor had some problem. He had also inquired of a passing Villager about the condition of the road ahead. It was quite a hopeless task of making to the next town at this dead at night. He asked me if I would like to take shelter in a nearby temple until the morning. There seemed little choice.

I collected my essential belongings and slowly made to the temple, which was half in ruins. I went in. With the help of torchlight I started looking around. The carvings under thick layers of cobwebs seemed ethereally bewitching.

I could not imagine ever seeing any one so enchanting as that Apsara who was beckoning me with her finger tips. Yes indeed she was calling me toward her. I heard a mystical voice singing a most lyrical melody. This voluptuous danseuse was seductively and gracefully moving her limbs to that tune. How could I resist, as she held my finger tips and gently pulled me toward her? She smiled flashing her teeth like a string of pearls and pealed out laughing. I was completely beyond myself. I could barely muster enough courage to ask her who she was.

She said 'Don't you know me? I am Parvati'. She had such strong resemblance to my filial relations.

And I said, 'It is nice meeting you Parvati. Do you see my car broke down? I am cold, hungry, wet and tired. You must know, I am in no mood to indulge in dalliance with you'.

Parvati started laughing again and slowly put me to her bosom. She ran her fingers through the shock of my hair gently stroking the scalp. 'Yes of course. You are such a cute little boy. Come, I will take you home'.

We slowly walked toward this neat little cottage. There was firewood burning in the mud stove. She said there was hot water in the bathroom with oil and shikapowder. I must have a good oil bath and change to dry clothes, while she made some nice hot meals. I did her bidding.

Even as I was drying myself in the bathroom, I could get the aroma from 'Murungakka' Sambar whiff past my nostrils. Before I sat down to eat, I started salivating at the look of that Mysore Rasam and an array of gastronomical delights awaiting me. She was frying for me those inimitable Thalli and Pori Vadams. I wished so much, she would sit by my side and keep feeding a morsel of the food on my palm, as my mom used to do. But that would have been so unbecoming of a big boy like me. Finally followed Rice, Curds and Vedumangai pickle. It all tasted divine. I have dined at some of the finest and most exclusive gourmet restaurants across the globe you could not buy a feast like this for the price of a King's Ransom.

I started licking my fingers at the last course and then finally managed to find my voice to ask her, "Who are you and why are you so nice to me? Before we let this go any further, do you have a husband or boyfriend or 'Significant Other'?"

She giggled ostensibly tickled. "You naughty boy, you are so sweet and likeable but hardly a match for me. You and I have never met before but we have a long and strong bond. Yes you will soon meet him. He always works late".

"Him? Who is he? Tell me about him".

I could see her face flushed pink with bashfulness and embarrassment. She first dropped and then slowly raised her demure face. With eyes still looking down she said, "Well, I could not normally take his name in public. But I could tell you. He is Veeraraghavan, I fondly call him Veeru in private".

"Oh Yeah? I guess he calls you Paro!"

"That is right. How did you know?"

"I am not so stupid as you think. I know all about you. When you met this new fellow, you dumped your earlier boy friend who is heart broken and now getting drunk in the den of a dancing girl down the street. Right?"

"I don't know what you are talking about. You are getting it all mixed up. Nothing like that happened here".

"Okay. Tell me about this Veeru of yours. How and where did you meet him?"

"Well one day I had gone to the river. After taking a bath, I filled this brass pot with water and was slowly walking back home. This handsome young man came on a horseback. He seemed lost and asked me for the way to Melalathur".

"Oh My God! That is the oldest line in the book and you fell for it? Then I guess he said 'What is a good girl like you doing in a place like this? Can I buy you a drink?' dah dah dah, one thing followed another. Right?"

"Hey Kid you must shut up and not keep interrupting me. You are wrong again. He got down from the horse and we walked together for a distance and I showed him the way to Melalathur. He said he was thirsty and I gave him water from my pot. Yes we did get friendly and got to like each other".

"But Paro, I hope you don't mind my calling you that, this guy is just a passer by. You know how these men are. He will just leave you and go away wherever he came from. Then what happens to you?"

"Now it is my turn to tell you, I am not so dumb as you think. He was coming from a very far away country called Wallahjahpet. I told him in no uncertain terms that I was not going to move out of Ananganellore. If he loved me, he had to move here".

"And he agreed?"

"Sure did. What do you think? He moved lock, stock and barrel".

"Bravo! He must be one full-blooded romantic hunk. But even then, are you telling me that you fell for the first guy that came along? Don't you want to get to know other men before settling down with one?"

"Oh My God! What a terrible thing to even think about? We women in these parts don't do things like that. We stick with only one man with a pure heart and soul, for eternity".

"Now Paro darling, are you telling me that women in your family never messed around? Then how come you have such a light skin and brownish eyes?"

"That is because my maternal grand mother sat too long outside on full moon nights and drank a lot of milk".

"Oh!! C'mon Paro, do you really want me to buy that baloney? You think you can get away with that? Haven't you heard of DNA testing? I can sit in the moonlight all I want but would never get any lighter than this. Are you sure those soldiers of Robert Clive's army did not go on flings in this village?"

"Of course not. We have had light skinned people for over a few Millennia, even before the Europeans arrived on those ships. Besides why would you want to get a lighter skin? You look so good to me, just as you are! Hush, now keep quiet, I hear my Veeru coming. You must meet him. He is really great".

Soon I could hear the hoofs of a horse. A tall, dark and handsome young man alighted. He and Parvati were locked in a close embrace and long drawling kiss, which seemed to last forever. My presence did not seem to matter to them at all. At last the young man turned around and saw me, still interlocked with his Paro. I could see a glitter in his eyes as he and Parvati started laughing again. Beaming with great pride, he told her I had his nose and cheekbones. Bursting with great love, she responded, for sure I had her eyes and jaw. They even agreed that my good looks came from her and the smarts from him.

I took courage in my hands and finally interrupted. "Just a minute you guys, cut it out. What do you think you are doing? There is decent company here. Parvati, does your dad know what is going on here?"

Parvati replied, "Why do you call me 'guy'? After gong to America you have forgotten good manners and good English as well. You have not come and visited us in a long time or bothered even to write. My dad has gone with the army of Tippu Sultan fighting the Marathas".

I jumped from my seat exclaiming, "Holy Molly!! So your dad is Subedar Anantharama Iyer, is he? I have heard about him from my brother. Why didn't you say that sooner?"

I quickly realized my *faux pas* and figured, it was time for me to beat it. Who would want to come between Paro and her Veeru, thereby endangering his own creation?

I heard footsteps of Murugan. I woke up rubbing my eyes. He said the weather and road had cleared. We were all ready to head toward Vellore. I could barely pull myself away from that dazzling Apsara.

As we were driving away, I asked, "Murugan, is this a car or a time machine?"

He said, "How do I know Saar? I am not even alive. You need to travel another 10 years down this road and ask someone".

EPILOGUE

Following is the lineage from Subedar Anantharama Iyer down to the Author:

Subedar Anantharama Iyer
—Daughter Parvathi/married Veeraraghavan
—Son Srinivasan/married Meenakshi
—Son Parasuraman/married Saraswati, Savithri
—Son Arunachalam/married Sundari, Sundari
—Son Subramaniam/married Sundarambal
—Son Arunachalam(SCDore)/married Chellammal
—Son Rajkumar Dore

All this is recorded on the Family's Genealogical Table Volumes 2 & 5.

It is true that the clan originally resided in Wallajahpet. A young man from there traveled and fell in love with a damsel in Ananganellore. On her insistence he moved to her village. With small stretch of imagination it could be assumed that this 'Full Blooded Romantic Hunk' was Veeraraghava Iyer, especially since the thread of lineage breaks down when drawn toward his family.

For those who don't know, Wallajahpet, Ananganellore and Melalathur are within a radius of 15 long miles, in North Arcot district of Tamil Nadu.

Robert Clive came to India as a GI for the British East India Company in early 1700's and left as the first British Governor General. He is credited of being the architect of the British Raj, his famous Battle of Arcot being a turning point.

Later he was tried in the British Parliament for multitude of wrong doings including cheating and embezzlement. He was however acquitted of all the charges. Speeches of Lord Macaulay in his favor and Edmund Burke against, are considered masterpieces of English oratory.

He had attempted committing suicide twice before in his lifetime. He tried again after his acquittal and succeeded the third time.

Finally, I just referred to an Encyclopedia and found Tippu Sultan acceded the throne of the Mysore Kingdom in 1782.

This might give the Reader a milestone of time in history when this imaginary encounter could have taken place.

<u>THE END</u>

PARADISE LOST & PARADISE REGAINED

INTRODUCTION

Partition of India and Pakistan had a profound impact on the 1st and 2nd generation Dorés. I think the brunt fell on my middle order siblings, Gullanna in particular and Giri next. They were in their critical formative years of their lives and this Tornado played havoc. I escaped with minor bruises. By the time I started growing up, our family had weathered the storm.

In the following pages I have tried to describe those critical days and the aftermath. This is from my perspective, in my words, as felt and remembered by me.

I would like to make it clear that this is intended to be more like a painting than a photograph. It is not a historical chronicle. Just a picture of feelings. Everybody likes to see his /her own name mentioned while reading. Some very important members of the family circle may find their names absent. This is not to belittle the importance of such people in our family relationships. That is because I am only touching people and incidents that are pertinent to the theme at hand. I am trying to only narrate important milestones of the family history in the setting of the Partition and its aftermath.

I have some times used names and nicknames for persons as known to me. To clarify, following are the Names and Relationships of the Characters in the narration:

Name	Nickname	Relationship to me
S. C. Dore	"Appanna"	My father
Chellammal	"Akka"	My Mother
Sundarambal	"Amma"	My father's mother
Kalyaniammal	"Kalyanathai"	My father's youngest sister
Vijayammmal	"Vijayamchitti"	My mother's younger sister
Dattatri	"Dattanna"	My brother number 1
Vishwanath	"Vichanna"	My brother number 2
Ramnath	"Ramanna"	My brother number 3
Prem	"Premanna"	My brother number 4
Gokal	"Gullanna"	My brother number 5
Giridhari	"Giri"	My brother number 6
Nirupama	"Roopa"	My sister, Sibling number 7
Rajkumar	"Babu"	Myself
Mukhi Mangharam	"Mukhi-sahib"	My father's Employer & dear friend

The other names in the narration are quite self-explanatory and consistent.

The narration consists of following two parts:

1. *PART ONE - PARADISE LOST; (Years 1940 thru 1950);*
2. *PART TWO - PARADISE REGAINED; (Years 1950 thru 1960);*

PART ONE - PARADISE LOST

Pluto Discovered:

I hail from a South Indian Brahmin family. We are not supposed to even eat eggs because it is the life of a potential chicken. After marriage my parents had a son, then a son, yet another son and so on. They wanted very much to have at least a daughter in the family. After 6 sons they finally got a daughter. They felt God had answered their prayers and now they must stop. They started practicing 'safe period, rhythm method'. After a while my mom, Akka complained of severe stomach cramps. For obvious reasons, it was first suspected that she was probably expecting a baby. In those days there was no sure way of knowing at such an early stage. After preliminary exams, doctors diagnosed it as Appendicitis. A day before the planned surgery, she was taken for a routine x-ray exam. It was found that she indeed had a baby as well. She was told that this was going to be a race between the inflamed appendix and the baby. If the former won, it would kill the latter and also Akka. The safest course would be to abort the baby, remove the appendix and save her. But Akka said 'No way'. She was willing to take the risk. In the final stages of pregnancy, she was put on liquid diet, mostly glucose water, so there is little pressure on the inflamed Appendix.

Akka had the baby. The Appendix was removed later. She lived to be 90. And I am that baby.

I was born at 4:30 AM on July 29th, 1940 at Hyderabad (Sind). According to South Indian Hindu Astrological standards, day begins at Sunrise. So they recorded my birth as 28th of July and that stuck all the way.

I found out recently from one of my brothers that my parents were quite hopeful, if not confident that I was going to be a girl. They had probably thought, they had it all figured out the right technique of making baby girls. I could imagine the looks on their faces when the nurse unfolded my diapers and they found it was yet another son. Pretty double crossed, that's how they would have looked.

Pluto is the last of the planets in the Solar System. For quite a while Astronomers had indirectly concluded its existence from the gravitational effect it had on other planetary motions. But only when very strong telescopes could be built, that its existence could actually be confirmed. Appanna drew a parallel and called me 'Pluto'.

I am really very proud and blessed, that my parents made a conscious and I am sure, a very agonizing, choice of having me against such odds. Isn't it amusing that even when I was created, they forgot to put me in the main Book and had to add in the Appendix later on?

Early Years:

I of course do not have the foggiest personal knowledge of any of these events and am totally oblivious of them. For me all this is just hearsay.

The earliest memory I have is that of my eldest brother Dattanna's wedding. I was barely 3. It was the first wedding in the family and was celebrated with pomp and circumstance, for full 5 days in Madras. Orthodox Hindu rituals and Social parties in 1943, when the WW2 was raging and there were rationing of all commodities. That was a moment of great pride and joy for the whole family. It seemed like everybody was having a great time, excepting the groom, who had not yet completely recovered from a bout of typhoid. But that was of minor reckoning.

I remember the new addition to the family, the new bride Kamakshimanni. She and Dattanna had a separate bedroom upstairs. One day I was standing outside her room peering through the half open doorway, as she was brooming the floor. I was too shy to go in. Seeing me, she bade me to come in and asked what was I staring at. I asked her feebly, why was she brooming the floor? She asked 'Why not?' I said, 'You are not Chandrika, are you? '. Chandrika was our servant who did all the cleaning and washing. She pealed out with a big laugh. Later she kept repeating this incident all over the family and they would also burst out with a guffaw and laughter.

Along with Chandrika, we had Ramraj who was my male nanny. Jagatram was our Chauffeur. Then we had gardeners and a retinue of servants to take care of every need. Our house was next to the PowerHouse of which Appanna was the Chief Engineer. He could command just about any thing he wanted and get it carried out by a hundred and odd people working for him there. We had a big house on the banks of Phuleli, a tributary of Indus River. The large lawn overlooking the river was well kept and we would play, go down the slide, seesaw or hang from the overhead parallel bars. Once Giri broke his arm trying go from one rung to another on those parallel bars. Karthik too fell from the seesaw and broke his collarbone. At that time there was a very popular song by KLSaigal that went "*Jab Dil Hee Toot Gaya*". And we would change it and sing for Karthik "*Jab Collar Bone Toot Gaya*"!!

We had some half a dozen cows and there were servants to take care of them. They were like our household pets. Akka would personally go and visit them every morning and some of them would even stand up and return her soft gentle stroking, with a grateful nod. When a cow fell sick, she had to be given medicine. A thick bamboo would be split on one end into two. After putting that end into the cow's mouth, a stick would be stuck in between that split, to keep that end and the cow's mouth wide open. A servant would place the medicinal pill inside the bamboo on the other end and blow with his mouth. Thus that pill would land straight into the cow's throat. However, sometime the stick keeping the other end apart would break and the cow would blow first, landing the pill inside the throat of the servant!! I guess that kept the servant quite immune to any disease as well!

In November 1944, we got the big news by telegraph that the first grandson had arrived. We placed a long distance call from Hyderabad (Sind) to Ernakulam. One had to book the call and wait for hours together before it would come through. Finally we could talk. We wanted to hear the voice of the new arrival. So we asked them to pinch that little fellow to hear him. Yes indeed that was true. Yes indeed that was the voice from the next rung of Doré ladder.

Karthik, as he was called, was an apple of everybody's eyes. At last I could now stand taller to someone junior. Appanna would show him around to his friends and colleagues with great pride and joy. Appanna's mother Amma had become a great grand mother through all male lineage. Quite an accomplishment by Hindu scriptural standards. That was commemorated by a ceremony called Kanakabhishekam - showering with nothing less than pure gold itself amidst chanting of Vedic hymns by a band of sacred Brahmins imported from far away South India.

After being tutored at home by Appanna's assistant Jiwa, for a while, I was finally admitted to the Nursery section of Pigget's High School near Tilak Chadi. We had a dark blue Ford convertible, four-door sedan that would take me to and fro school.

One afternoon in early 1946, Appanna picked me up from my school and we drove back home together. All else had already finished their lunch. Keshavan laid a wooden board on the floor and a plantain leaf before it. He served Appanna his lunch in our traditional style of partaking meals. I sat separately and as usual was creating a ruckus to finish my food. Akka brought the mail and there was a letter from Madras with a picture of a 16-year-old petite, comely girl with large beautiful eyes and shapely neck. She passed the letter to Appanna. I asked them who was in that picture. I was told, that was going to be my new sister-in-law. Things started ticking like a well-oiled clockwork. Within a few weeks, in June of the same year, we were in Madras for Vichanna's wedding to Sarlamanni.

By early following year, they were expecting their first child. In the traditional South Indian Hindu fashion, a celebration called 'Sheemandam' was celebrated in Hyderabad. It is similar to what the Westerners call a "Baby Shower".

In the school we were taught to draw the Union Jack for our assignment. I would use the kitchen knife to draw all those lines criss cross. Then one day, we were told that we did not have to do that anymore. We were to draw the tricolor flag of Independent India. Just 2 horizontal lines, fill Red, White and Green, with a round wheel in the middle. That should be easy enough.

Calm before Storm:

Yes India had become Independent. I had no idea what that meant. They made Karthik wear the closed neck long jacket and tight trousers called Churidar. With Gandhi cap to top it all, he looked very cute and like those Congress leaders in newspaper pictures. Flags were unfurled and people constantly listened to speeches on the radio looking pretty pleased with themselves.

While all the States, some two thousand plus of them, were asked to choose between India and Pakistan to join, there were a few that created more problems than the others did in making any choice. Amongst such was a tiny state called Junagadh in Gujarat whose Nawab stubbornly wanted to stay away from either. Whenever I used to throw up a temper tantrum without eating my meals, Keshavan our cook would call me 'Junagadh'!!

Our home was an oasis for the South Indian community in that part of the World. Being some 1500 miles away from Madras, most of them, especially the bachelors, considered this their home away from home. They would come to celebrate festivals like Dusserah, Deepawali or Avaniavattam, the annual day to change one's sacred thread. They may even drop in on weekends for no reason at all. They may even telegraph us to meet them at the Railway Station with coffee and meals when they were en-route some place else. Amongst a host of such friends were Mr. Subbaroyan, who later was the Editor-in-chief of "Sind Observer", a daily in Karachi. And then there were Captains Srinivasan and Balu, of the Indian Army.

181

We got a new car. The old Navy Blue Ford convertible was still there. But we prided on the new Chocolate colored Ford with a stick shift below the steering wheel. I still preferred the old car because it had that extra step below the door that would help my small body to climb in and out. But nobody wants your opinion when you are not even 7 years old. Our schools closed a few days of opening, after the Summer Recess in 1947. There was trouble brewing all over the region, so parents wanted their kids to stay home. Akka would tutor us in the Tamil language to keep us stay away from trouble and to get some training in our mother tongue. Punjab in the north had started having serious communal clashes between the Hindus and the Moslems. All kinds of horror stories were being reported in the media. Hindus were fleeing in droves across the border. The foreboding was, that someday this cancer was going to spread towards Sind, where we were living and was thus far quiet.

All our belongings especially the valuables were shipped across to India with Captains Srinivasan and Balu. Being bachelors, they did not have much belongings of their own and were very willing to carry our stuff as their own. None could mess with the Army personnel on the way.

The Exodus:

From our house we could see trains going over a railway bridge across the Phuleli. They would be overflowing with fleeing people holding on to every nook and cranny of the compartment and over the roofs, hanging on to their lives literally. My playmates and their families would come bidding good-byes. Every man, woman and child wearing six or seven layers of clothing. They could only carry what was on their bodies, if they even made it across the border alive. Feria Sahib and his family could stay on, they were Christians. Bhise Sahib a Hindu, Mohan Singh a Sikh, with their families, were in peril.

We always thought this whole black cloud will one-day just pass away. 'This is not really true', 'This couldn't be happening to us', 'All those terrible things you read about in the newspapers only happen to 'others' never to ourselves'. Denial. Denial. Denial. One day Appanna, rang up Subbaroyan in Karachi to find out just how bad the things had gotten and what precautions, if any, should we be taking. Subbaroyan was fuming like the Vesuvius. He flared out at Appanna. He could not believe we were still lingering there. He told in no uncertain terms that we must get the hell out of that place immediately if we did not want to be raped and killed!!

That is when the whole reality dawned. All means of transport were chock full not to mention fraught with danger and disaster. Subbaroyan, with his journalistic contacts was finally able to wangle seats on a ship called "Jala Durga". She was a vessel salvaged, reconstructed and making her maiden voyage. That is all that was available. No First Class seats. Just Upper Deck. Take it or leave it. We grabbed 8 tickets: Appanna, Akka, Amma, Kalyaniatthai, Gullanna, Giri, Roopa and myself. Keshavan, the cook got a place in the servants quarters.

Late night on November 23rd, 1947, we took the train from Hyderabad to Karachi. Next morning after reaching Karachi, we heard the news that after we left that night, communal riots had broken out a mile away from our house and Hindu houses were set on fire.

Appanna paid some Rupees 250 to the Coolie for loading our dozen or so trunks at the docks. That was equivalent to US$ 10,000 in today's terms. We were lucky we even got such a bargain. Around 3 PM on November 24th, "Jala Durga" slowly steamed out of the harbor. Subbaroyan along with some of Appanna's loyal colleagues and friends was standing at the shore waving at us. There was no eye that was dry. There was no throat without a lump. One momentous chapter of our lives was slowly drifting away from us like quicksand under our feet. Our minds stopped registering any more emotions, it had just reached its limits. The land we were forsaking slowly but surely turned into a blimp on the horizon. We heaved a sigh of relief choking with sadness. A veritable oxymoron indeed.

Appanna was able to get leave of absence from his employer and old time dear friend Mukhi-sahib, by promising that he would return after safely depositing women and children at home. There was still a lot of work to do. The two of them had worked shoulder to shoulder in their shirtsleeves for the better part of a quarter Century. Appanna had created and nurtured that PowerHouse like it was one of his own kith and kin.

The Holocaust:

The carnage and conflagration of Partition was close to what the Sub-continent got to a Holocaust. Our family came within a kissing distance to it. We came out physically unscathed. Tens of thousands of others were not so fortunate. Horror stories abound and history books are full of them.

Much later, I had a roommate called Ravi Kant Shrivastava who related to me an experience in his family when they were in Lahore at that time. His dad was a Professor at the University there. One Sunday morning, Professor Shrivastava was walking down a lane ending into a cul-de-sac. He was late for a visit to his friend in this predominantly Moslem neighborhood. One of his students, a Moslem, yelled at him from the balcony of his house, beckoning him to come inside his house immediately first. Notwithstanding protestations, the student dragged the Professor into his house and locked him up in a closet. A little later he was let go. He was then told that, the previous night all the people in that neighborhood had decided that the first Hindu that walked in would be slaughtered. Professor Shrivastava would have been that person. A Hindu teacher was saved by his Moslem student from being butchered by other Moslems!.

It was a mass frenzy. To any right thinking person, it made no sense at all. If 'A' killed 'B' on one side of the border, 'C' killed 'D' on the other side, for revenge as well as a deterrent from 'E' killing 'F'. Who started all this first? Don't bother answering that question. Husband would be tied to a pole in the railway station. In front of his eyes, throats of his child would be split open by bare knife. His wife would be raped, before her breasts cut out and strewn on the floor. His parents would be cut into pieces. After witnessing all this he would be untied and killed too. A little boy of his would probably escape to come and tell the story to others. These were not just stray incidents. There were thousands of such incidents taking place in broad daylight all over.

Pakistan was a wholly Moslem state. Hindus settled in Pakistani territories had to be uprooted. They no longer belonged there. But India declared herself secular. Families were thrown apart as they fled. We used to hear broadcasts on the All India Radio, separated families trying to find each other. *"Vishwanath, Shikohabad sey poochtain hain, Akka, Appanna, Gullu, Giri, Roopa aur Babu, Kahaan hein aur Kaisay Hain*!! ". ("Vishwanath from Shikohabad seeks to know where and how are Akka, Appanna, Gullu, Giri, Roopa & Babu") When you heard your name being announced like that, you were supposed to go to the nearest police station and let them know your whereabouts.

The only entity that could and did bring some semblance of sanity was Mahatma Gandhi. He fasted unto death in Calcutta and stopped the carnage there. However he was assassinated by Nathuram Godse on January 30th 1948. We were in Bangalore and that evening at about 5:30, within half an hour of his shooting, a cousin of ours told us as he heard about it on his way in the bus. We even did not have a radio at home to listen to the news. We had to rush to some neighborhood house. I was too young to understand what had happened. I was asking everybody who was this Mahatma Gandhi and whether he was bigger than the King was. Every body was fretting and fuming to even bother listening to my questions. They were all talking about how he was shot by a revolver, whatever that was. It seemed like the whole nation wept for his death. Even our own family members observed fasting until his body was cremated next day. Ashes were distributed a few days later in schools that were brought home in small packets for people to put a speck on their foreheads and touch on their eyelids with solemnity.

With Mahatma Gandhi's death things could only turn worse. Riots broke out again. Rashtriya Swayam Sevak Sangh, a Hindu volunteer organization was blamed for the death as well as for fomenting religious bigotry, rightly or wrongly. Ramanna was a strong sympathizer of this organization and was an undergraduate student at Anand in Gujarat. He was telegraphed to come home immediately as he would have been in danger of being in harm's way. One could not say what was in store next, for the country and our family.

To give you a historical perspective, it was the time when: King George the VI was the Monarch in England, Harry Truman was the U.S. President, Europe was in shambles and Marshall Plan had not yet been announced, Don Bradman was the Captain of Australian cricket team, the United Nations was still functioning from Lake Success UT, the state of Israel had just been inaugurated, a very young singer called Lata Mangeshkar was struggling to get her first song recorded.

The Dilemma:

Seven days after leaving Karachi harbor, our ship arrived in Bombay. After taking railway trains, we finally made it to Bangalore.

We landed at my aunt Vijayamchitti's house on 11 Nehru Nager. She had rented out half of that house and was living in the other half with 2 sons and 3 unmarried daughters. She declined Appanna's offer of monetary compensation for our stay with her. He used every other opportunity to make good her hospitality.

After a couple of weeks, Appanna wanted to go back to Hyderabad (Sind) and start where he had left off. To Akka and others that seemed like an insanely suicidal thought. He wanted to go keep a promise he had made to his friend and colleague. To others it seemed like jumping into a quicksand or burning house to save a friend. It was a moral and ethical dilemma for which there is no easy judgment possible.

Of the seven sons and one daughter, only the oldest two had semblance of being settled. I being the youngest was still only 7 years old not yet in the primary school. Appanna's chances of coming back alive from that Inferno was very slim if at all. Should he or should he not go to save a friend from his predicament?

Mukhi-sahib wrote letters beseeching Appana's return. At least 2 of those were intercepted by Akka and not given to him until later. Appanna was understandably very upset. There was commotion in the house and a furor in the family. Appanna packed up and was going to leave for Hyderabad (Sind), regardless.

That was when Akka got into hysterics and decided to go on a hunger strike until, either death or Appanna rescind his decision. The tussle went on for nearly 3 days. Akka lay in her bed without having eaten even as much as a morsel of food.

Finally Appanna had to give in. He decided not to return and wrote to Mukhi-sahib of his decision. Mukhi-sahib felt betrayed and very disappointed and wrote him so. It was a long time before the two could patch up their friendship.
This dilemma can be perceived from the perspectives of the three people directly linked.

I feel Appanna's main motivation for wanting to go back was indeed to keep the promise he had made to Mukhi-sahib. But that was only one of the several reasons.

He was also totally and completely in love with the PowerHouse where he had spent almost 2 decades. He had built it from scratch, nuts and bolts, to finally rise to be its Chief Engineer. For him that Power House was almost as much part of his life on the one hand as his wife and kids were, on the other. Between the two, it was a very intractable choice he was being forced to make. He thought he could get away having them both.

He was also a person who dedicated himself a cent percent to his work, making him almost a workaholic. Work was for him a 24 hours a day, 365 days a year involvement. For a long time later on, he would wake up at the middle of the night sweating, thinking that some transformer somewhere needed his attention. He would still hear telephone ringing or generator pounding when we were 1500 miles away from the PowerHouse. To make such a person sit idle and read newspaper every morning was a cruel punishment he could not suffer.

He had been a highly respected person with a lot of power and prestige. The kind of treatment he was getting in Bangalore then was a total travesty.

All these factors put together made him almost obsessed with the idea of going back without regard to the risk he was putting his family and his own life into.

From Akka's perspective there was indeed very little she could have done by way of leveraging her opinion on his decision. Her intercepting the letters from Mukhi-sahib was indeed wrong. But that was because she was in a quandary. No straightforward and correct method may have worked. In any case her ploy did not last long nor was it material. She did have to finally hand over the letters to him and face the consequences. For her too, having a good comfortable life with a steady income, power and prestige, was just as important as for others. But she was able to weigh it against the risk of Appanna not coming back alive at all. She could have been widowed with 6 unsettled children and a modest nest egg.

Ideally they two should have locked themselves up in a room and discussed this matter like mature and rational adults with Mukhi-sahib's letters on the table. They should have confronted each other boldly, weighed all the pros and cons and come to a final decision no matter how unpalatable to either.

On the part of Mukhi-sahib, as a true friend, he should have understood the risk he was putting Appanna into. He should also have understood Appanna's family responsibilities, predicaments and limitations. Mukhi-sahib did finally wind up the establishment in Hyderabad (Sind) and come back to settle down in Bombay. Appanna and he met after many years and reconciled their differences to patch up their friendship.

But after 50 years, all that is so easy for us to say and be judgmental. The mechanics of relationships and circumstances were so different then. We can only draw lessons from it now. We may face similar dilemma ourselves in our lives and do much worse.

The Village:

I don't know what was really going through his mind, Appanna every now and then would threaten me that he would send me away to mind goats and cows at the ancestral village, if I did not study and got good grades in school. One of the alternatives he probably considered for himself and his family was to go back to the ancestral village and take up farming on lands of his paternity, that he had left back several decades ago.

One of the most memorable weeks of my life, was the one that I spent in our ancestral native village of Ananganellore, in North Arcot district, in the state of Tamil Nadu in India. I was 8. Appanna took me along, when he went to inaugurate the first electrical water pump at our farm there.

The nearest railway station for the village was Melalathur, where only Passenger trains running between Bangalore and Madras, stopped for just 2 minutes. About 15 miles away was a major railway station of Gudiatham, where all trains including Express and Mail, halted for 10 minutes. Gudiatham was also the district head quarters.

The only mode of transport between our village and the Melalathur railway station was a bullock cart belonging to one Moslem called Ghaffur. By profession, he was probably a tailor or a tiller, but he doubled as the Director of Transportation, being the only taxi driver in the Village. In a typical vernacularization of the name, he was popularly called 'Ghaffoorawn'. We had to inform him ahead of time to meet us at the railway station for a particular date, time and train. A normal post-card costing half an Anna (16 Annas made a Rupee) would take about 7 days to reach from Bangalore, if at all. So, considerable planning was mandatory if we did not want to be stuck after alighting from the train and trek our way home carrying the luggage.

Our Passenger train arrived on time. Yes there was the ever-obliging smiling face of *'Ghafforawn'*, waiting to receive us. The two mile journey took us some 2 hours, with all the jostling and rattling of the ill fed bull pulling us at its own sedentary pace. The village had one main street called Brahmins' Agraharam.

It ended at one end with a temple as cul-de-sac. The first house from the temple was that of the Priest. Ours was the second house. There were about a dozen or so houses on both sides of the street. Beyond that, there were farms as far as eye could see. On the backside of our house, flowed the river of Palaar, if and when it ever had water flowing. At the time we were there, in the middle of summer, the river was no wider than a 3-ft canal that we could jump at one stretch.

As the name indicated, this was the street of the Brahmins. Others were not allowed to come on it. We had a sharecropper called Bhupalu working on our farm who was a '*Pariah*', an outcaste. Even when Appanna would ask him to come to the front of the house to talk, he would be too awe struck to do so.

We reached home late afternoon. We had to finish eating our dinner before sunset. I had never been in a place that fell dark after sunset and people moved around with hurricane lanterns. Electric power had just been introduced to that village, but only for farming purposes. There was not enough to go round for unnecessary luxury like lighting the houses. Ours was the first electric pump in a radius of at least 25 miles. People just could not believe that water could be really pulled from 50 feet below in the dried out well, without any human or animal effort.

At the appointed day and time chosen as auspicious by the Astrologer, all people of the village gathered around the well. After the rituals of offering coconuts, flowers, plantains and a lot of prayers to Gods, Appanna finally pushed the magic button on the wall. There was first a gurgling and grinding noise of the wheels churning. Then after a suspenseful pause of a couple of minutes, water started to gush from the pipes straight on the faces of the people waiting around with skeptical looks. The joy, surprise and total bewilderment felt there, are beyond description. People purposely came in front of the gushing water just to feel the spray, dancing and singing. No such thing had ever happened there before. Real spring of water in the middle of hot dry summer. Yes, indeed "Eagle had landed".

At the end of the week we packed up and left for Bangalore. We walked across the dried up Palaar, jumping that 3-foot stream holding on to our dhotis. On the other side was a bus station called Kuthambakkam. A rural bus would come every other hour, laden with all kinds of people oozing sweat. After loading our luggage on top, we had to huddle inside with those zillion people pushing and shoving us. We finally made it to Gudiatham to catch an Express train. That District was in the Madras Presidency. And our home in Bangalore was the Mysore State. We were not allowed to take agricultural products across the border. We would do that any way. We would tell people at home to wait near the railway line for the train we were coming by. As the train passed near our house, we would roll the bags of rice and other stuff out of the train.

The Pits:

Appanna had built a house on 12 Nehru Nagar in Bangalore. Way back in 1940 lots of land were being sold cheap in this undeveloped outskirts of town. Akka's dad Bachappa bought one, her sister Vijayamchitti bought one. Akka cajoled Appanna into buying one in between those two lots. He even built a house on it without knowing that he would ever use it for living. He wanted a house there just to spend holidays or store unwanted luggage. But later, that house was rented out to New India Pharmaceutical Co. They were quite prompt in making their rental payments. But they were using the house for the manufacture of pharmaceuticals that spoiled the floors and walls. They were also unwilling to vacate the premises, now that we wanted to come and stay there. The court system favored the tenants and it was no easy task to get them to go. Besides, the court system was ridden with red tape and corruption.

After staying with Vijayamchitti for some 6 months, we finally moved into our own "Meenakshi Nilayam", as the house was named. Amma and Kalyaniatthai had already started living in our ancestral village Ananganellore after we came from Hyderabad(Sind). So it was just my parents, Gullanna, Giri, Roopa and myself. Ramanna and Premanna were at Navrozji Wadia College in Poona, working on Bachelor of Science.

Vichanna was working for Bajaj Glass Works in Shikohabad. He got his first child Mridulatha. Some wanted to name her Swatantra, being born 2 weeks after the

Independence. That was the first granddaughter of the family. Girls have always been very treasured in our midst.

Dattanna was working near Ernakulam and got his second son Ganesh. Named so for having been born on Ganesh Chaturthi day.

Dattanna would come every now and then to generally be of help and assistance. He was instrumental in getting Gullanna and Giri admitted to the St. Joseph's Indian High School in Bangalore Cantonment. That was considered quite a good convent school for Indian boys. There was still a St. Joseph's European High School meant only for Whites. Their school was some 5 miles away from home. On weekdays they would get a school bus to get there. But some times they would have Extra Classes over the weekends or they may miss their bus. Then they had to pack their rice-and-curd in tiffin carrier and trek all those 5 miles. So they both got bicycles. Gullanna a regular size and Giri a smaller one.

Smaller it may be, but having ones own bicycle clearly put him in a higher category. He could even stick two fingers inside his mouth and whistle like a railway engine. What good was I? Would I ever be good enough to ride a bicycle? I told myself, if I ever grow up and make a lot of money, I would open a big school for all little boys to learn riding a bicycle. Cycling was easily the 3rd best choice for my profession after Airplane Pilot and Railway Engine Driver.

Giri had a very mean teacher. Once Giri fell sick and submitted his homework assignment one day too late. The teacher asked him to go sell it in the Russell Market. We all gave that teacher fellow, nickname 'Russell Market', then on.

Roopa joined Kamala Bai's Girls' High School along with Vijayamchitti's daughters Chingariakka and Mythili. It was quite a conservative girls-only school. I could never figure out what kind of a person this Kamala was, if she was both Boy and Girl? Why would my sister want to go to a school named after such a weirdo? But when you are barely 8, you know you are much smarter than these older folks are, but your ideas and opinions just don't count. The elders just get by, riding roughshod over your immense wisdom by brute force. That was for sure. Like any nice girl hoping to get a good husband, she was given training in playing the Veena. Her music teacher would come every other day and the whole house would be full of noise. Sooner or later even I started to develop a taste for Carnatic classical music. It is hard not to do so, when you are held hostage to so much good culture thrust down your throat every other day. Psychologists call it the Stockholm Syndrome, I believe. Being the next younger sibling and a male, it had become my role to play her chaperon. Any time all the people had to go out when it was her tuition time, I had to stay home. You could never say what these music teachers could be up to.

On our backyard a couple of Car garages were turned into a school for little neighborhood kids. I was sent there. After a few months I moved to another better school, Arya Vidya Shala, a mile away by foot. I started learning Kannada. I first had a tutor at home who was just too mean. He would make me read from a book and just doze. Then he would suddenly wake up, call me very sweetly to come close to him. As I would go near him waiting to be appreciated, he would yell "My dear fellow, how come you have no brains whatsoever?" Once Akka caught him catching me by the ear and twisting it hard. That was the last we ever heard of him in our house. Then I got another tutor that was much better, except that he had the habit of using nasal snuff powder all the time and sneezing it on a handkerchief that needed washing very badly. I started liking the new school and had some good friends. My grades were generally picking up.

After we moved out, Vijayamnchitti rented out half of her house to one Dr. Rama Iyer, an Ayurvedic doctor. He had boys of my age group, called Balu and Cheenu. We used to play cricket on the dusty road in front of our house and generally hang out together. I asked Balu once to teach me how to whistle like Giri did. He wanted 10 matchbox labels to do that. Despite bargaining and negotiating, he would not bring the price down below 8. There was no way I was going to pay that kind of a price. My matchbox labels were really of very superior quality and rarity. Ask anyone. At that tender age itself I learnt that technology did not come cheap and people who have it do not part with it easily. So I decided to go on my own. I tried hard to imitate what they were doing. All I got at the end of my effort was a lot of snort from my nostrils and bloated sinuses. I decided that whistling was not the be all or end all of life. Did Alexander the Great whistle when he was young? What about Erroll Flynn or Vijay Merchant or Frank Worrell? They were no whistlers either. They did pretty well in their lives did they not?

All this was a far cry from the kind of life we were used to. We thought people here were very mean and rude. The family savings were dwindling. Appanna thought of all kinds of avenues to keep himself gainfully engaged. He even applied for the job of a Meter Reader in the local Power Company. He was disqualified for he was over-qualified. He wanted to put his remaining savings into a Restaurant business. That was too risky and none of us knew anything of running a restaurant. Then he decided to put some money into building another floor above our house so it could be rented out.

The contractors and masons were again hard to get by. They were all totally corrupt and crooked. They had to be watched constantly and sometime things had to be done ourselves. Gullanna would go on his bicycle late at night looking for some wood or steel bars and then saw them for window frames. Crime and burglary was a constant threat. Once even as we were all at home, the house was burglarized at the middle of the night. The cops were totally incompetent and sometimes hand in glove with the criminals themselves. Even ordinary things like getting firewood for hot water or grocery for kitchen, had become one big relentless juggernaut. There was no decent mode of transport. The local buses were undependable, overcrowded and inconvenient. There used to be horse drawn carriages called Jutka. That would jostle along forever and haggling with that driver at the end of journey was more stressful than the whole journey itself. After a lot of thinking we finally indulged in the luxury of buying a radio. Paillard, a Swiss make multi-band Short-wave radio.

In the middle of all this it was found that Appanna had diabetes. Once he was walking barefoot on the front yard and stepped on a rusty steel wire left over from a cracker during Deepawali festival. That wounded his foot and caused septic. In a course of time it got so bad that the Allopathic doctors decided that his foot would have to be amputated. That was indeed a very agonizing possibility and it seems Appanna even considered ending his life rather than do that. Then Dr. Rama Iyer next door took a look at it and asked if he could get a chance to cure it. He applied some indigenous leaves and pastes. Within 3 days everything got healed like nothing had ever happened.

The upstairs was duly completed and let out as two tenements. We lived in half of the downstairs portion. The remaining half of downstairs was also let out as two tenements. That brought in some steady income. We were not destitute by any means. But there had been a precipitous fall in our living standard and style.

This was going on and on for months without any end in sight.

Then finally after more than 2 years of our coming to Bangalore, at the end of 1949, a letter arrived from long time friend called Chandan Singh Bharkatiya, now living in the city of Indore.

END OF PART ONE

PART TWO - PARADISE REGAINED

The Backdrop:

In early 16th Century there was a Palace Revolt in Chittorgarh, the Capital of the Kingdom of Mewar. All members of the royal family were killed, excepting one. Infant prince Udai Singh was in the care of his wet nurse Pannadhai. She was looking after him along with her own infant son, as she heard the stomping footsteps of the on coming soldiers approaching these portions of royal chambers. The Usurpers wanted to eliminate the last of potential challengers to the throne. With great presence of mind, Pannadhai wrapped the little prince in a blanket and placed into a basket. She replaced him with her own infant son in the royal crib. After planting one final loving kiss on her own son, she fled with the basket.

Prince Udai Singh grew up incognito in the jungles and trained to become one fine soldier. He was able to raise an army with the help of his loyal followers and other nomadic tribes. Then he started looking for a place to establish a new capital city from where he could campaign to regain his lost kingdom. He traveled some 90 miles west of Chittorgarh and found a spot that was ideal, as if ordered by him. In the middle of the Aravalli Hills ranges was a large lake Pichola. He tied his horse to a stone by the lakeside and looked around. He knew then and there, that was his most perfect place. He was going to build heavy stone gates at strategic entry points to the valley, to prevent and be forewarned of unfriendly intruders. He would place observation posts on hilltops. The lake would provide wherewithal for any prolonged siege. The thick jungle blanketing the hills and valleys would also provide perfect hideout for his fledgling army. What more could he have asked for? Thus the city of Udaipur was founded.

All the kings who succeeded Udai Singh built on what he had found first. They consolidated his gains by building more dams across the valleys to collect rain water into large reservoirs. To establish their authority, they built fortresses and palaces across this territory of nearly the size of England. However they were constantly struggling to maintain their independence from Invaders and Empire-builders from outside. The Maharana, as the kings of this state were called, made a treaty with the British, when the British subjugated the whole sub-continent. The Maharana was allowed to keep his internal autonomy pretty much intact. His government was even allowed to mint its own coins, which were valid legal tender along with the Indian currency. In return, a British Resident was allowed to stay in the city, who acted as the 'ears and eyes' of the British Crown. Defense and External relations were within the overall jurisdiction of the British Viceroy.

In the 1920's British King George 5th held a Durbar at the newly inaugurated Indian Capital of New Delhi. Along with the other Indian Maharajahs and Nawabs, he invited Maharana Fateh Singh of Mewar. The Maharana was going to be conferred the titles of GCSI (Grand Commander Star of India) and KCIE (Knight Commander of Indian Empire). It was also symbolic of all the attending Princes accepting the hegemony of the British Monarch by paying their obeisance. In the last four Centuries, Maharanas of Mewar had taken the vow of never going to Delhi and offer obeisance to any Emperor, not even to the Grand Moguls. Was the Maharana going to do that now? The Maharana politely informed of his inability to attend the Durbar due to 'indisposition'. The British sent an Emissary to deliver the titles to him at Udaipur. The Maharana gave audience to the Emissary and received the honors. After the Emissary left, His Highness directed that the Sash and Insignia be put on his favorite horse.

Maharana Fateh Singh was very wary of foreign influence on his Kingdom. He guarded age-old traditions very jealously. He himself moved around on horseback when outside his state, people used for transportation a new innovation called automobile.

One night the Maharana went to bed wondering why the soup he had for dinner tasted a little different. He never woke up to find out the reason.

Short-circuit in the Network:

Fateh Singh was succeeded by his son Bhupal Singh to the throne. He was mentally very competent but was paraplegic below the waist, being a victim of polio in childhood. The new Maharana was more liberal. He opened up his territory to some modern technology. He laid railways connecting Udaipur to major cities. He built roads and imported cars. Besides opening schools and colleges for boys and girls, he also introduced electricity by establishing a Power Utility company named after him. That was primarily meant for supplying electric power to his palaces. Excess capacity was sold to general public. As the demand for electricity started to grow with the growth of the city, his government soon realized that they could not manage this company efficiently by themselves anymore. They invited bids from outside parties for buying and managing this company.

Suganmal Bhandari was the Chairman and principal stockholder of Nandlal Bhandari & Co., in Indore. This company was basically in the Textile industry. They were looking for opportunities to diversify and expand into other territories. With lots of construction activities going on in Udaipur, they wanted to get a foot inside the doors of Maharana's government, so they may exploit business opportunities there. With this in mind, they put in their bid for this Power Utility company, even though they had no experience in that field. As luck would have it, their bid was accepted. They were landed with this baby, with which they had no idea what to do. Suganmal happened to mention his predicament to another business friend of his Chandan Singh Bharkatiya, while making polite social conversation. Chandan Singh responded by saying, he knew just the right person who could help him out. Thus came about that letter from Chandan Singh to Appanna at the end of 1949. Appanna went to Indore in response. After meeting with Suganmal and Chandan Singh, in January of 1950, he accepted the position of Chief Engineer and Manager of Maharana Bhupal Electric Supply Co., Ltd., in Udaipur (Rajasthan). When he returned from Indore, Appanna came laden with presents for all of us. I saw the card in the leather writing pad he brought for Akka. It read "To TDO". The acronym stood for "The Dear One". He went to Udaipur alone to take over his new charge and make arrangements for rest of us to join him. Our schools were still on and the annual exams would not be over for another 3 months. On April 24th 1950 we all boarded the train from Bangalore for Udaipur. Happy days were going to be here again.

Putting the Pieces Back Together:

We started regaining the old luster in our life-style. We had a nice house with servants, cooks and car with chauffeur. In the beginning this place was so unspoiled that they even had not heard of that ubiquitous scourge called Income Tax. People were very simple minded and innocent. Vegetable vendors did not know about weighing and counting. You handed over a fistful of coins and she would shove a big handful of vegetables into your bag. The monarchical system had imbibed a sense of respect and awe toward all those wielding power and influence. It was considered rude to look at a person of higher standing in his eye when talking to him.

The changeover from Kannada medium in Bangalore to Hindi medium in Udaipur was quite hard on us at school. Giri, Roopa and myself had a private tutor at home to make this transition easy. He was a direct descendent of Goswami Tulsidas. For those who don't know, he wrote the Ramayana in Hindi considered a Masterpiece of literature. He is considered the Shakespeare of Hindi literature. Our teacher, Sri Ganesh Puri Goswami, as he was called would knock off one mark for every word we used that was not Hindi in its utmost purity. Getting him to sign off our homework, with his characteristic 'GA-PURI', at the end of the day would win us our daily wings.

Dattanna had moved to Burnpur near Calcutta, having got a position with Indian Iron & Steel Co., there. Ramanna was working on his Law degree at Poona. Premanna was in the Medical College at Madras. All the rest of us were at Udaipur. Vichanna had moved from Shikohabad and was now running his own glass bead factory. The others were in college and schools. Dattanna wanted Kartik to bond with his grandparents and learn family tradition. So he was staying there too. When we sat for dinner it was a room-full. At around 9 AM it was a mad rush for all of us to get ready for the day. We would all try to get into the bathroom at the same time. When we got into the car ('loaded ourselves' would be a more appropriate expression) it would be like a can of sardines.

There was a kind of double facet to our personalities. Inside the house we maintained a typical Tamil Brahmin orthodox tradition. We ate on the floor, only a Tamil vegetarian cuisine. Observed all the rituals and festivals. But once we stepped out of the house we had to mingle with our North Indian friends and colleagues. The language we spoke was a mongrel of Sindhi, English, Tamil, Kannada and Hindi. Which language dominated, depended upon what we tried to emote. Our language of profanity was developed only in languages that were spoken outside home. We remained so illiterate when it came to abusing in Tamil.

This dual culture manifested itself in various forms. Akka would want us to go abegging on 'Porattashi' Saturdays. On those four Saturdays in the month of 'Porattashi' we had to don silk dhotis, wear a 'naamam' on the foreheads and go seeking alms. We had to eat only what we collected in charity. This is supposed to be an exercise in frugality, humility and penance. However being what we were and the school bell ringing at 9 AM sharp on Saturdays, we would go 'abegging' in our chauffeur driven limousine!! Akka would call 4 families ahead of time to keep our alms ready. We would get down from the car, costumed like clowns and pick up our 'alms' that would be kept ready for us. After finishing our round of 4 houses, we would hurriedly rub off the makeup and change into 'civilized' clothes in the car itself before rushing to the classroom as the bell would ring. In the school of course the environment was quite different. We spoke, sang and learnt everything in Hindi and sometimes in the Mewari dialect.

In 1952 we celebrated the 60th birthday of Appanna. We invited our family priest Ranganatha Shastrigal from Vellore. Aunts, Uncles and Cousins from all over came. The house was full of fun and frolic. When people talk of 'quality time', that is my idea of it. When we went seeing movies, we had to book one full row from one end of the hall to another. And there were those endless picnics and outings.

Udaipur has a typical Tropical climate. Some 10 weeks of summer stretching from May till end July. At this time the temperature easily hits 110 F or 40 C. In those days A/C was an unthinkable luxury. Most people stayed home during days with blinds drawn on all the windows and doors. We would sleep on the terrace during nights after sprinkling water on the floor. With cool breeze blowing from the lakes, it would be just heavenly. Come end-July or early August, we would have the first sprinklings of Monsoon rains. It would rain heavily for a few days. Then it would sprinkle off and on till the end of the year. All the lakes would be full to the brim. The surrounding hills would be blanketed by greenery all across. Peacocks would start crowing and dancing in the woods. It would be a common sight to see them spread their dazzling tails even from our own windows. That would be the time when the whole landscape takes on a most beautiful sight imaginable. People would celebrate the season by having Fairs, Dances and Music. There is something about Folk Music. It does not follow any set rules or need special training. It comes straight from the hearts and souls of people. As if from the soil and earth itself. It penetrates straight into the depths of your sentiments. The percussion beats and soulful tunes have that pristine and primeval human flavor that is hard to define. That is what makes it such an important part of the whole environment. It touches you right within your vital parts. The whole area becomes so beautiful that it has been a favorite haunt for moviemakers to shoot their films. We have met several of them including Vyjayantimala, Dilip Kumar and Shashikala etc. It is also a favorite place of other celebrities from India and abroad to come for their private vacation. There are any number of most picturesque spots for outings and picnics.

By now the political landscape in the country was also slowly changing. New Constitution had been inaugurated. The erstwhile princely states were all consolidated into Federal States headed by Governors. In 1952 first General Elections were held for Federal and State governments. I recall Jawaharlal Nehru's visit to Udaipur on a campaign trip. We were at the airport reception for him. There were throngs of crowd all over, trying to get a glimpse of this national hero. Appanna, Ramanna and myself did not want to get jostled by the surging crowd and were quietly standing at one corner of the tarmac. And to our utter surprise, Nehru came walking in our direction as he was taken on a detour from the main crowd. We not only got to take a good look at him but also shake his hand and exchange pleasantries. A little later as we were trying to get back into our car, we found that Indira Gandhi had got separated from her dad and got mixed up with our section of the crowd. As she was trying to get back into Nehru's jeep, a policeman not knowing who she was, was trying to beat and push her back. At his point Ramanna stepped in and played the chivalrous Sir Gallahad. She finally got on the jeep and waved us good-bye.

Empty Nest:

Around this time Vichanna decided to wind up his bead-making factory as he had a job opportunity in Bombay. However after taking up that job he was not very happy with it. Appanna had known a German friend called G. Wilhelm from back in Hyderabad days. He had come to Appanna as a Sales Engineer from Siemens of Germany selling Siemens turbines, before the WW2. However during the war he had been imprisoned as a citizen of enemy country. After the war was over he along with 3 other partners started a company called Protos Engineering Co., which were the agents in India for Siemens as well as other German companies trying to re-establish their business. They were expanding and needed a good dependable work force. Appanna renewed his friendship with Wilhelm and sent a letter through Vichanna. Thereby Vichanna got a position of Sales Engineer with the Siemens in Bombay.

Along with Roopa's wedding I also had my Upanayanam in 1953. Later Appanna and I returned to Udaipur while Akka was still behind winding up and taking care of some other chores. On our way we stopped at Bombay and paid a visit to Wilhelm at Protos Engineering Co. Appanna wanted to personally thank him for the help he had given Vichanna. That was the first time I also met Wilhelm as Appanna introduced me. Appanna also bought me my first wristwatch, during our halt at Bombay. As we tried boarding the Frontier Mail at Bombay Central station, we found that there was a mix up in our First Class reservation. The Travel Agency asked for berth in the name of Mr S. C. Doré. In the telegram 'S' of the initials got attached to "Mr" and they reserved a berth for "Mrs" C. Doré in the ladies compartment!

By 1953 all the birds had flown away and the nest in Udaipur had become almost empty. Roopa had got married and lived in Bangalore. Gullanna had joined Engineering College and Giri joined Commerce College in Bangalore. They were staying in "Meenakshi Nilayam" with Amma and Kalyaniathai. Ramanna and Premanna were still studying at Poona and Madras respectively. So that left just me and my parents at home. I was in High School now.

After appearing for my High School exam in 1955, we all went to Bangalore for Roopa's first confinement. I got my Roll Number all fouled up. When the results were announced in the newspaper, everybody home thought I had flunked. Appanna was in Udaipur and found out from school that I had really passed with good grades. He wrote a strong letter telling me that just for that reason, I deserved to be flunked!

Appanna would invariably score 20 out of 20 in the "Readers Digest" Word Power quiz. Once he got 19 and after referring to the dictionary we found Wilfred Funk had flunked! We could hardly come up to that kind of record, but we tried. At home we were all strongly encouraged to read books. In fact if you wanted to appreciate and understand the conversations at dinner time, you had to be quite well versed with various quotes and anecdotes from

PP ("Pickwick Papers") or P&P ("Pride and Prejudice"), besides, PG Wodehouse, Dickens, Alexander Dumas Oliver Wendell Holmes, etc. There was always a large stack of books in our library at home. Very early on I realized that books are my best friends. There is nothing in this world at my level of information, that somebody has not already thought of and written a book about. Whenever I had a question or was curious about something, I could always pore over a relevant book to figure out the answer. Books never talk back at you. They never tell you your question is stupid. They don't tell others behind your back about what questions you asked and spread embarrassing rumors. Whenever Appanna went on business trips I would ask him to get me books. My favorite authors at that time were R. K. Narayanan and Pearl Buck. Along with my books Appanna would also bring a bunch more. My school would finish in the afternoon by 4 and when I came home there would be nobody. I would normally curl up with some book. Once I found a book on "Marriage and Sex" written by a couple of very recognized medical professionals. Appanna had brought it on his latest trip. I sneaked and read that book from cover to cover, when nobody was watching. Now looking back I realize that I was not outsmarting my father. That is exactly what he intended me to do! We never could have a frank conversation on matters like this. Instead, he bought that book and just put it in the shelf so I would read it behind his back! Otherwise I don't think at the age of 65 he would have bought that book for his own reference! I believe that was pretty smart of him. That was my father, my hero. "Talk by your deeds, not by words", "Keep your eyes and ears open but mouth shut", he would say.

Task of Sisyphus:

Soon after assuming his new position in Udaipur, Appanna realized that it was not for nothing that the erstwhile owners of the company wanted to get it off their hair. It was ridden with all kinds of problems and Appanna had to shoulder them. The Company had been running at a loss and money was being constantly sunk into it just to keep it afloat. It had no system of administration. The people working there had neither any technical nor managerial talent. The power generators were old and inefficient. It was a typical catch twenty-two situation. The company could not become efficient and profitable unless more money was invested into it. The parent company was reluctant to pour more money into an enterprise that was already running at a loss and they had not intended to buy for keeping anyway. There was constant labor unrest as people working there were not happy with low wages and poor working conditions. When the company tried to get out of the financial mess by increasing the price of electricity, the consuming public raised hue and cry. Power Utility is a highly visible industry and touches every person on the street. Thus local politicians and the government officials were willingly participating in the fray taking sides in warring factions. There was also a very huge credibility gap amongst the public, labor, government and the parent company. Appanna was right in the middle of all this.

Building trust and confidence is the key to any situation where there is such an amount of chaos and disorder.

For example if there is a fire in a theater with a huge crowd trapped into it all the people can be saved if there is one person at the exit that they all trust to maintain order and let them out in an orderly manner. If not all the people would try rushing out at the same time and all of them would court disaster.

Another example would be when there is a run on a bank. Due to some rumor if there is a panic and all depositors withdraw their moneys from a bank at the same time, the rumor becomes a self-fulfilling prophecy and the bank does in reality collapse. Somebody needs to step in and shore up the confidence level of the depositors for the bank to stay afloat.

Appanna's task was similar. It took him quite a while to gradually win the confidence of the investors, consumers, labor and the government. And that process was very arduous and also fraught with danger to his personal safety. There were times when there was all out strike by the trade union. His office was surrounded by placard holding and picketing laborers. He was kept locked up in his office for several hours. There were times when the public was in a rage and his car was surrounded by a crowd while on his way to work with hecklers trying to manhandle him. But in such situations, it was his undaunted pursuit of truthfulness and fair-mindedness that pulled him through. Slowly people started to like him and even trust him as a person. But at that point the adverse factions wanted him out of the way so they could fly at each other's throats and pull each other's hair!

There were also suggestions that the company be taken over by the government. To pull the company out of this morass, the government had to be convinced that no matter who runs it, the price of electricity had to be increased to generate real resources. Having done that, the investors had to be convinced that the extra resource had to be ploughed back for buying better and more efficient machinery to produce more electricity cheaply. Then the real profits had to be shared between the labor and consuming public.

At this point there was one local politician called Mohanlal Sukhadia who rose to prominence and held the position of the Chief Minister in the Rajasthan government for record number of years. For him keeping the city of his home constituency happy and prosperous was of paramount importance for political survival. Electric power is the basis for every other economic development he had in mind. The old cliche goes, "There is no Power as expensive as no Power". He himself figured out that taking over a company that was being managed as best as it could be, was not a smart idea. He wanted the company to expand and grow, along with the growth of the city and all the new plans he had in mind. As a matter of fact, Sukhadia not only wanted Appanna to continue the good work he was doing in Udaipur but also nominated Appanna to the Consultative Committee for the State Electricity Board, so his knowledge and experience could be utilized for other projects, government had in mind. Appanna was also nominated for the State Productivity Council and was given medals of honor.

By around the middle of 1955 it seemed like the dark clouds hovering around Appanna's work were slowly clearing. Even then he would put some 16-hour a day and 7 days work week.

Pinnacle of Glory:

In 1955 after graduated with a Bachelor's degree in Commerce, Giri was going to start working on Chartered Accountancy with a firm Appanna knew in Indore. Meanwhile Vichanna informed that Siemens were looking for three fresh graduates to train in Germany for 3 years before being absorbed in Management cadre. That was a golden opportunity and Giri left for Germany in January 1956. We all were terribly excited about the whole event. That was the first 'Doré' to set foot outside the country. Giri got excellent reports there. His weekly letter home was a family event we all would look forward with eagerness and excitement all week. We would sit around as Appanna would read it to us and we would be looking askance.

Next to go overseas were Vichanna and Sarlamanni. They were in Germany too and came back with a whole lot of slides of Europe and gifts for all of us. Tape Recorder was a great novelty then. We were quite fascinated at listening to our own voices played back.

1956 was also eventful for we got our first 'Doctor in the House'. Yes Premanna passed from Madras Medical College with good honors and our pride went up one more notch. He had made all arrangements to go to Edinburgh and then to London for doing his MRCP. He came to

Udaipur to spend some time before departing overseas. Even his passage on the ship had been booked. There was a certain amount of nervousness on the parts of Appanna and Akka at one more son, especially a doctor son, going away for so long when their own age was advanced and health was uncertain. To make things worse there was a crisis in the international scene as Gamel Abdel Nasser of Egypt nationalized the Suez Canal and there was an imminent danger of a 3rd World War breaking out. With all this Premanna's going to Edinburgh got postponed and then canceled altogether. He got a job at the General Hospital in Udaipur itself.

Around this time our family had reached its zenith. We had gained a lot of stature in the society. While our family was known for Appanna, it was now also being widely recognized for Premanna. In fact there was hardly anybody in the city and even state wide, that was not some how or other touched by either. Akka had her own circle of friends and so did I. We were members of local country club. Even though Appanna himself was not the clubbable kind, we used to make full use of it with his membership. In a town of about 100,000 people we were one of the just a half a dozen family that became highly respected and recognized. At the end of a typical day we would all sit together or get into the car for a drive around the Fateh Sagar Lake, exchanging our day's happenings. Premanna's experiences in his medical world would never stop amusing us. If nothing else, he would tell us all about a 'fantastic' case of some latinized name for heinous medical malady. We would all wonder how such an abomination could ever be 'fantastic'.

There were times when Premanna and I were left alone at home with only the local servants who did not know any South Indian cooking. We asked Akka to give recipes and directions in writing. We experimented with cooking ourselves. We only had problem in getting the right proportions of different ingredients. The outcome was not always all that bad. We exhausted Akka's year's worth of grocery stocks in about a month in this process of learning by trial and error. Once we made Pudhina Chutney and left it on the grinding stone as we forgot to bring to the dining table. Next morning we found a rodent quite dead near that stone. It is still a mystery if our Pudhina Chutney was the cause. If we could figure that out we could have got a patent for pesticide.

Premanna's wedding to Prabhamanni took place in 1959 at Madras. We had taken some servants from Udaipur for help. One of them was Kishan Singh who knew no word of Tamil and was also one eyed. In the afternoon of the Wedding Reception, all the male members were having a siesta on the floor of a big hall. The groom woke up with a start and remarked that the trousseau for that evening's gala was all crumpled and needed ironing. I woke up hearing that and said my suit needed ironing too. I volunteered to take his and mine to a nearby laundry. Slowly each man woke up rubbing his eyes and wanted to join the fray. Before long I was entrusted with the onerous task of getting a dozen suits properly pressed. I went to the laundry along with Kishan Singh carrying the load of suits. I got the groom's suit pressed first on top priority and sent it back with Kishan Singh, as we were already quite late and dignitaries would have started arriving. I was to follow with the other suits after they had been done. When I reached the Wedding, there was no sign of Kishan Singh and the groom's suit. At the appointed time we were all dressed prim and proper, excepting the prima donna, who was still in his underpants! Kishan Singh finally showed up an hour late. There were half a dozen Wedding Receptions in the neighborhood that evening. He had lost his way and was looking for us in the wrong wedding. He could not even ask anybody for directions, as nobody would understand him. Moral of the story: Don't mix an important assignment with a bunch of less important ones. You may call it a corollary of Murphy's Law.

Our parents had set a goal for all of us. They wanted that every single one of us must complete a Bachelor's degree at the very least. Better if we chose to go higher. They never forced a choice of any particular profession. We were pretty much free to take any subject or line we felt comfortable with.

After we returned celebrating Premanna-Prabhamanni wedding in September 1959, I went to Jaipur to attend the Convocation ceremony at my University there. I received my degree of Bachelor of Science. I came back and showed my picture in the gown and hood, bearing the rolled up scroll in hand. Appanna and Akka were sitting together. Appanna took the picture from my hand. The expression he had on his face is still frozen in my memory. The gray eyebrows over his eyes were knitted. He had that glazed look on his wrinkled face. Was it pride, joy, sense of accomplishment or just relief? May be all of it. He was not a person that was easily moved to tears. He could barely control a couple, ebbing in his eyes. That was of joy and happiness. It was not so much of a degree for me. It was for the Shepherd and Shepherdess whose last sheep had finally romped home.

They must have felt like marathon sprinters having finally made it to the finish line. That was a long sprint from where we were ten years ago.

THE END

ABOUT THE AUTHOR

Raj Doré is a Software Engineer hailing from a very orthodox South-Indian Brahmin family. He was born in Hyderabad (Sind), now in Pakistan, before the Partition. When the Indian sub-continent was divided, he and his family fled to India. He migrated to the United States in 1977. He now lives with his wife Sumita in Dallas, Texas, U.S.A.

He has B.Sc. (Mathematics, Physics & Geology), MA (Political Science) and MBA. Later he worked on MS (CS) at the Southern Methodist University, Dallas, Texas.

He is a member of MENSA and INTERTEL, the high-IQ societies. His writings have been published in their magazines as well.

He has traveled widely in Europe, South America and Asia. He knows English, Hindi, Tamil and German.

www.ingramcontent.com/pod-product-compliance
Lightning Source LLC
Chambersburg PA
CBHW030311290526
45785CB00001B/299